There Is a GOD, and I Am NOT HIM

Reality vs. Perception

BRITTENY LAVONDO

ISBN 979-8-88685-107-6 (paperback)
ISBN 979-8-88685-108-3 (digital)

Christian Faith Publishing
832 Park Avenue
Meadville, PA 16335
www.christianfaithpublishing.com

Printed in the United States of America

PREFACE

This book tells the story of a young girl who was almost lost. She grew up in a household where she felt as though she was unwelcomed and unloved. She had various trials and tribulations which shaped her. But because she believed that things were bad, *her reality became her perception* which means that things went from being bad to catastrophic in her mind. As you all will begin to read, you'll see that she is quite a character, telling her story from different points of view, using poetic methods, and relating to things like food, movies, books, and TV shows. She even used a time machine because she goes back and forth in time. She tells her story from a child's point of view, but then she grows up. You'll see, for she is *me*.

INTRODUCTION

Someone once said, "To be successful we must go through the pain, find our passion, and walk in our purpose." Reality vs. perception:

There were many that looked like her and quite a few that came before her. She was a brown-skinned woman with nine siblings. Because she was closer to the baby child, on most days, she got what wanted physically but did not get what she wanted emotionally. Her life struggles and determination turned her into the "beautiful woman."

My Beautiful Woman did the best she could with the tools she had, with the next generation. She was the youngest of three with high hopes and big dreams, a smile that could stop traffic, and eyes that could see through to the soul. Her hands were always cold as ice, but her heart was warmed as coffee topped with cinnamon and whipped topping. During those times, it was hard for her to differentiate reality versus perception. She has a brother who is the oldest, a sister, who is the middle child, a loving mother and father.

I was different from the time that I could remember. I kept to myself, keeping one to three friends by my side. My eyes watched every move. My mind calculated every step. With that being said, I did not talk much growing up until I talked. My grandmother always said, "You can learn exactly who a person really is by simply watching them." So I watched and watched. I waited and waited to see if I could recognize the flaws, imperfections, and the cracks in people. I would quickly learn, I would quickly see, I would quickly recognize the demons that surrounded me.

My mom was the only person besides my dad that I cared about. My mom was this beautiful woman. She was the peanut butter to my peanut butter cookies; she was my star. And the only thing that I ever wanted was her approval.

When things took a turn for the worst, they really took a turn for the worst. My life was quite different because I did most of it alone, at least I thought I was alone, learning how to live, learning how to love and be loved, learning how to be forgiven and to forgive, learning how to face and accept hardship, heartache, and headache (the triple H).

CHAPTER 1

Family

Every day, living in that household to me was considered a "beat me up" or "break me down" day. Every day, I would get up from bed, and the sun would smile right down on me. It was as though someone or something was watching over me, allowing me to go through things, maybe even preparing me. I would often smile back at him saying, "Another day," "When will the days become the nights for me?" "Who am I?" "Why am I so important to you?" "Am I good or evil?" "Why won't my mother love me?" "Why does my sister want to kill me?" "Why doesn't my brother care about me?" "Where is my dad?" I would continue with my day knowing and accepting that it always would start off pretty, then get ugly, and finally, it would become something ridiculous.

This beautiful woman was gorgeous to me. Every man wanted her, and every woman wanted to be her friend. She was multitalented with the ability to do hair, makeup, sing, dance, and she fit into every type of crowd. I would often watch her do her makeup in hopes that one day, I would become as beautiful as her. Every weekend, this beautiful woman would hang out with her friends, leaving us with family members that "loved us so much" that they beat us until pain became the norm. If we smiled, we were beaten. If we thought twice about something, we were beaten. If we cried, we were beaten. Well, I was the cry baby, so I was always beaten, then subjected to the room or the place where the bed was. Those days I didn't know that what

I was going through then would affect my life now. I would often imagine myself in an hourglass filled with sand, with time elapsing, hoping that someone would save me. Some days, I would imagine someone tying me up, then pouring Redpop! all over me, and slowly torturing me until death. Death called my name and called my name until one day, I started reaching for him, scouting for him, SHOUTING HIS NAME in hopes that he would find me.

Often, I would stick to my mom like molasses. Once I latched on, it was hard to get me off. I hated for my mom to leave because I had found comfort in rubbing her legs. It was the only time that I could feel compassion, and it reminded me that something besides myself was physically there. (This was kinda like the movie *Inception*. He would spin top, and if that top stopped spinning, then he was in the real world. But if it kept spinning, then he was in a dream.) Most days, it felt like I was in a dream. Anywho, She had opposing feelings toward it. She'd often say things like I was going to be gay, or it made her feel nasty. But, boy, was she beautiful. Her skin was like milk chocolate, smooth all over. Her hair was like the sea. It was wavy. Her body was like a coke bottle, perfectly formed. And her personality was like deep fried chicken. Everyone loved it.

Those days, I was so alone that I found a friend. This friend, she went everywhere with me. She slept with me. She ate with me. She even listened to my every thought. She was always there for me. She played with me because no one else would. When the mind is beautiful, who can change it, a loved one perhaps? The other children would not accept me because to them, I was weird. To her, I was perfect. Dee Dee kept me calm. She was my release. She was my family, and she was my hope. She is the reason that I am the person that I am today. She taught me the importance of being patient. And she helped me understand the idea **that people may think they are by themselves, but no one is truly alone.**

As a baby, I had an umbilical cord infection. This caused my navel to smell something like rotten eggs. That smell lasted for many years. So it wasn't that my family did not want to be around me. It was that they couldn't tolerate the smell. I had thought that they did not like me. Unfortunately, I did not have that revelation until I was thirty years of age.

My sister, she was the Boss. She had the Boss' look and attitude. But when I say she was gorgeous, I really mean gorgeous. She looked like she was black and Chinese mixed. Her hair often high-fived her butt cheeks. It was that long. Her face was completely rounded, with eyes so tight we'd often questioned if she could see. To top it off, she had a body to kill. "She was bad."

My brother was the golden child. He could do no wrong, with a mocha-skin complexion, eyebrows like bushes, teeth that needed no correction—until he thought he was Superman—and a personality like our mother's. He resembled my uncles; therefore, he stood tall and confident. He often kept to himself.

> So God created man in his own image,
> in the image of God he created him; male and
> female he created them. (Genesis 1:27 ESV)

CHAPTER 2

Dee Dee

I didn't have the attitude like my sister, nor did I have confidence like my brother. But I did have Dee Dee. At first, Dee Dee was comforting. She was my friend. But then she slowly showed her hand. She let me know that she wasn't who she claimed to be. See, she wanted all of me. She became miss negative Nancy. Relationships, whether family or friends, were of nonexistence. I would go to school, and she would tell me that people were saying bad things about me. She told me I was better off by myself because no one would accept me. She said my family did not deserve me and that she could make me happy. She would often tell me that I was not the little girl she had met years ago, that I was changing.

I don't remember how Dee Dee looked. But do remember the way she made me feel and the things that she said. One thing she said to me stood out. This thing stood out because it was intentional. It was as though she became all those people who hurt me. It was as though it wasn't me that was changing but her. She said, "No one would ever love you because you are ugly and weird." This was a different type of pain. This pain was not physical, but it was so much more. I told my AO (best boy cousin) the whole story. He listened and waited until I finished.

He whispered in my ear and said, "Who is Dee Dee?"

I said, "The girl that's always with me, the girl that I am always talking to."

He said, "No one is ever with you, and the reason why other kids won't play with you is because they see you talking to the air and to the walls." At that point, something hit me like a ton of bricks. All at once, I started to realize that he was actually right. No one could see her, and no one could hear her. Was she a spirit? Or pretend? Could she have been my imaginary friend? Dee Dee disappeared, to show never again. This formed a bond between my cousins and I. We had relations far beyond the eyes. It was out, it was in, but we were products of our father's sins.

> My God hath sent his angel, and hath shut
> the lions' mouths, that they have not hurt me.
> (Daniel 6:22 KJV)

CHAPTER 3

The Beast

Growing up, my mother recognized the loneliness that trapped me. Instead of talking about it, she put a Band-Aid over it. She gave me my first pet. It was an all-black cat with green eyes. When I saw him, next to him laid a black button, so his name became buttons. I rubbed his belly for about five hours, and from that point, I was his best friend. I fed him three times a day and changed his litter once a week. If I ate a cookie, he ate a cookie. If I had pizza with pineapples, he had pizza with pineapple. We became inseparable. We would watch movies together, and when I wanted a snack, he would share his food with me. *That darn cat.*

Buttons, he was something special. Often, my sister would be mean to me, and he'd scratch her on my behalf. Ha, ha, ha! I found humor in that. But he was something else. When he slept, he would sleep walk. He would stand on his hindlegs and bob and weave. We thought he was dreaming of getting a taste of his favorite meal, which was deep fried chicken. We would soon find out that we were wrong.

My school was directly behind my house. You can almost say it was in my backyard. So I would walk to school every day. But when I left the house, so did buttons. He would walk with me to school and find his way back home. When I returned home, he would always have a gift for me. Sometimes it would be a rabbit. Sometimes it would be squirrel, and other times it would be birds. He would be wagging his tale so cheerfully. And it never failed. He loved me enough to bring me something special every day.

One night, I fell into a deep slumber. Cold as winter's breath my body laid. Darker than dark is what I felt. Optical illusions going in circles over and over are what covered the room! Then it appeared, in somewhat of a human form to me. A throne is where it sat. It had a ring on every finger. One ring was the government's. One ring was the music industry. One ring was the movie industry. One ring was for cartoons. And the biggest ring of all was one of all the souls it had captured. It said to me, "Come home, my child." There I stood confused because I knew that I wasn't evil, but I was unsure if I was good. As I came to realization, I could not move. The room was still dark, and that same dark presence that I felt in that vision, there it stood. Out of nowhere, these eyes that I will never forget appeared—Big as the walls, red as blood, almond shaped, mesmerizing, capturing, full of pain, and death. They glared at me as though I did something horribly wrong. Then Buttons, my hero, ran into the room and began to fight it. It fled from buttons as though he was a protector. It was soon known that Buttons was my protector. The calm before the storm was the atmosphere. Then peace entered, and soon he smiled down on me saying, "Good morning."

> Fear not, for I am with you; be not dismayed, for I am your God; I will strengthen you, I will help you, I will uphold you with my righteous right hand. (Isaiah 41:10 ESV)

Something about me that was the definition of different. Maybe it was the gentle and patient spirit that surrounded me. In that dark world, I was considered medium well. Many years later, I worked as a nurse aide doing home health care. I worked with an eighty-five-year-old woman. She was a Caucasian racist who absolutely despised African Americans. She lived in a $4-million mansion all by herself. It was beautiful. She had a full garden attached to her room with a slide door that allowed access in and out of the garden. She would always call me Monkey. "Hey, Monkey, get my meds," or, "Hey, Monkey,

I'm hungry, and I need to eat. And you better not poison me." Her comments did bother me. But by this time, I was "Army strong," so my skin was quite tough. But I noticed that every day that I went to her house, the roses would start to blossom. So one day, I simply asked her why she was the way she was. She told me that her whole family was killed thirty years ago in a car accident. And she didn't know why God allowed her to live. So I shed a few tears and told her that "I don't know why God allowed you to live, but what I do know is that you still have breath in your body. So you have time to ask for forgiveness." By this time, I had but a few more days at that assignment. And out of nowhere, all the flowers bloomed. I had never seen roses as big as pumpkins. The roses were almost the size of Seymour in the movie *Little Shop of Horrors*. She smiled and offered to treat me to lunch. **Life could throw you a curveball. And because your perception became your reality, it could take eighty-five years to heal. But don't give up because he won't give up on you. He has always been there and will always be there.**

> For ever since the world was created, people have seen the earth and sky. Through everything God made, they can clearly see his invisible qualities—his eternal power and divine nature. So they have no excuse for not knowing God. (Romans 1:20, NLT)

CHAPTER 4

Home

What was life like for me, being me, struggling with identity, socially awkward, with different strands of adversity? Being paranoid from the hip joint, born and raised in Detroit, it was a hard term, but it was the norm.

I wanted nothing but for that beautiful woman to say, "I know who you are, and I accept every ounce of you." But those days were quite different though. I was angry and felt as though the whole world owed me an apology. I felt like I was a permanent victim. When I went left, I found pain. When I went right, I found disappointment. When I went up, I found loneliness; and when I went down, I found darkness. The weight of the world was too heavy for my shoulders, but I wanted it to change, *waiting on the world to change.*

One night, it was the night before picture day, that beautiful woman did her daily routine. She would get off work and cook dinner for us that was ever so good, then tell us to clean, which took a lot of time, and finally, send us to a world that we only knew, dreamland. Mom was a transporter by day, counselor by evening, and mother by night. This day in particular, after dinner, I asked her if she could do my hair so that my pictures would not be scary. She said, "Baby, I have had a long day, and I am really tired." I said okay as my eyes filled with water. She then said, "How about I do a really pretty ponytail for you?" My eyes lit up like a kid in the candy store.

I had two ponytails, one on the right side and one on the left side, lopsided if you think about it.

Before I knew it, the Boss came in. She said, "I want my hair done too."

The beautiful woman said, "You don't have picture day tomorrow, and I don't want to even do your sister's hair." This was not acceptable to the Boss. No. No. No. She lit up like gas when fire hits it. She began screaming directly at her, telling her how she favors me, how she is tired of this, and how horrible her life was.

The beautiful woman's eyes began to water, and she said, "How do you want your hair?"

She said, "I want it flat ironed." At that moment, so many thoughts flooded my brain. I thought for sure that the beautiful woman was going to dig so deep into her that she would have come out a different person. For I thought that there is no way that she is about to flat iron her hair because she is tired. She put some crooked ponytails in my hair. And not to mention, I have picture day tomorrow, and the Boss does not. To my surprise, she indeed flat-ironed her hair; and for a few hours. I watched. **That night showed me that there could be ten people in the same household; and all ten of them could live different lives, could have different pain, and could turn out completely different.** For that night, I saw the hurt in our mother's eyes and the deeply rooted pain in my sister's heart.

What could the beautiful woman be hurting from? And what could the Boss be hurting from? With my family, I thought that I was the only one unsure about her identity. I thought that I was the only one who suffered that fate. With the procreational, could it have been generational?

> Thou shalt not bow down thyself to them, nor serve them: for I the Lord thy God [am] a jealous God, visiting the iniquity of the fathers upon the children unto the third and fourth [generation] of them that hate me. (Exodus 20:5 KJV)

Beautiful was how it began. Breakfast was served, the beautiful woman was happy, the Boss was quiet, and my brother was playing the game. Maybe he was thinking of the time when a police officer ran into our home pointing a gun at all the children, me to be included, and them rough handling him. I don't know, but the game seemed to keep his mind off of our lives. My brother was quiet, but his eyes were definitely open. Midday rolled around, and there was no change. They were still happy and content. My Aunt China came to visit, "with arms as wide as the doors" is what we used to say. It means full of love. She grabbed my mother and said, "Hey, sister-in-law." She grabbed my sister and said, "Hey, my beautiful niece." She grabbed my brother and said, "Hey, handsome." She looked at me and began to talk to my mother. She never acknowledged that I was in the room.

I was sad and later told my mother. This beautiful woman said, "Baby, you know that that's who she is." At that moment, thoughts began flooding my brain. Did this beautiful woman see what happened? Does she care about what happened? If she saw what happened, why wouldn't she take up for me? But then again, why would she take up for me? That night, my sister invited a friend over. Jessica was always sweet to me. And I secretly wanted to be like her. Jessica and the Boss were talking. Mom was out of sight but within a voice's distance. Brother was doing what he did best, playing the game, and I was sitting next to Jessica. They were talking about things that I was too young for. They were talking about BOYS. Yuck! Jessica had said something about how that boy was cute. My sister laughed and said, "He is super cute." Jessica then went into a hysterical laugh. But I knew the boy too and had felt the same way. So I said, "He is really cute." Jessica was still laughing. The Boss stopped herself from laughing with the quickness, got up, came over to me, and began punching me in the head, all while telling me how stupid I was. Maybe I missed something because to my understanding, they were talking about how cute the boy was. I screamed, I cried. I then looked up at Jessica, and tears were in her eyes, all while still very confused. I went to the room in pain beyond pain. I was emotionally hurting while really physically hurting. So I began to pray. I told the Lord that I did not understand, that I did not do anything wrong, that I was scared to be in my own home. I told him that I wanted to die, and then I thought, *Why should I have to die? It is her that must go.*

> We are hard pressed on every side, but not crushed; perplexed, but not in despair; persecuted, but not abandoned; struck down, but not destroyed. (2 Corinthians 4:8–9 NIV)

Weeks passed, and what a beautiful day it was. It wasn't too hot, too cold, or too rainy. It was still. There were no birds chirping, no wind blowing, and no one outside that we could see. Every time Aunt Lea saw me, she'd say, "There is my secretary of state." Little did she know I held on to that my whole life. She was my inspiration for going further. We had breakfast on the go with my Aunt Lea and her three children. The oldest was my AO. Our favorite diner was the National Coney Island. There we ate with laughter and enjoyment. My Aunt Lea had asked my mother if she could watch the kids while she ran an errand once we got back to the house. My mother agreed. Hot and crowded the house became with three of us, three of them, and my mother. We had a two-bedroom house. My mother then told us to go outside and get some vitamin D. We played and played. Finally, my AO suggested that we play manhunt. This game was just like hide-and-go-seek. The difference was that you can hide within a block radius, and when someone finds you, you must then help them hunt for the next man.

Pug was Auntie Lea's middle child. He hid by a bush two houses down. Before we knew it, he screamed for us to come to him. We questioned whether or not he was playing. He said, "For real, y'all come here." So we all went to him. He pointed out to us that there was a gun, a sawed-off shotgun. Scared as we were, we did not want it to get into the wrong hands. Pug picked the gun up. My brother yelled at him to put it down. He put the gun down, and we decided that it was too dangerous. So we headed home to tell my mother. The boys ran back to the house, waiting at the door for us. My sister and I walked back. There, I stood to the right of my sister, and a tree was to the right of me. The boys began to scream and point at something behind us. We could not hear them nor understand what they were saying. So we continued to walk. Before we knew it, a guy from down and across the street ran to the bush. He picked up the gun, aimed at the tree, pressed the trigger, and ran. I jumped with fright in my heart. Thank God, it was a sawed-off shotgun. Then I looked down, and blood was all over the concrete. I felt my body, and I was okay. But about eight bullets hit my sister. I felt as though my sister was not going to make it. My mother went into panic mode because of insurance and licenses she did not have. My brother said oh how he wished it was him and how he should not have ran off.

Hours went by, and we had no word on whether my sister was alive or dead. So I laid down to rest my mind, and something that was a voice and a feeling said to me, "Didn't you ask for your sister to die? Do you still feel that way?"

I said in a panicked voice, "No, No, No. If she dies, who is going to beat me up? If she dies, who is going to give my mother a run for her money? If she dies, who is going to pay for it? And who is going to replace the Boss? Surely it can't be me, I don't know how to be mean. PLEASE, PLEASE, PLEASE keep her, for she does not know." When I awoke, there he was smiling down on me; and everyone was crying but, not tears of pain, they were crying tears of joy. The Boss was going to live and have a full recovery. From that day forth, I never got that mad at my sister again.

> Death and life are in the power of the tongue: and they that love it shall eat the fruit thereof. (Proverbs 18:21 KJV)

CHAPTER 5

The Pain and Anger

Somewhere along the way, my perception became my reality. The way that I thought of my life became my life, fifteen years of being stagnant. One day, I heard a story of a woman. She was very healthy, and every day she'd look in the mirror and compliment herself. But one day, she had a doubt. She then felt bad, so she went to the hospital. They ran a test and found she had stage 3 breast cancer. They told her that she immediately needed to seek medical attention. She didn't understand. They told her that if she didn't go through surgery immediately, she would die soon. They scheduled her for surgery two weeks out. Her hair began to fall out, her skin began to change, and her confidence went down the drain. Her perception changed, which made her reality tough. **We don't know why God allows us to go through things in life. But what we do know is that life is a test. And you can either pass this test or fail this test. Even though we know the road to passing the test is narrow, we don't have a choice. It's literally life or death.**

Overcome the pain. Find your passion, and walk in your purpose. For your purpose can be found through the pain, and out of that, stirs up your passion. And that's how you know that you have found your purpose.

There it stood lying on the doormat. It was like a leech sucking the life out of me. It was so potent that all anyone would have had to do was just ask, and I would have told it all. I remember feeling like

I was a goldfish, and the world was full of shark tanks. I was always scared and worried.

In those days, my uncle lived in our basement. Uncle Wartholomew was not a bad person; he had just made a few left turns in his life. He was consumed with pain, so he found a Band-Aid to help him cope. This Band-Aid came from a leaf called "Coca." One day, my mother had all the children, including our other cousin DC. DC was the oldest known child of my mother's youngest brother. As always, when the house was too crowded, my mother told us to go outside.

On this day, we were bike racing. DC had a new bike, and all the children were obsessed with it. It was orange with black designs on it. The race was on. Whoever could make it around the block the fastest could hold the block championship for best bike rider. During the race, the rules were that two people would go at one time to prevent injury. It was my turn to ride with AO. Helmets and kneepads were in place. DC did the countdown. 1, 2, 3, GO, GO, GO. So we took off. The wind blew my hair, and light as a feather was what I felt.

We hit the first corner. The curve was steep, and rocks covered the pathway. My bike began to shake. My confidence began to deplete, and I knew I was going to fall. So I began to slow down and cry. AO then stopped and said, "What's going on?"

I said, "I almost fell."

He said, "But you didn't, so get up, I am counting on you." Out of nowhere, a spark of confidence entered my mind. I got up, and we hit the next corner, at about twenty miles per hour is what it felt like. The next corner was the home stretch. With all the strength our bodies had, we went as fast as we could. Side by side, we looked at each other and smiled because it was either going to be a tie or a very close race. It was so close that we could almost taste it. And then out of nowhere, a car came. The car just stood there. We had no way around it. We both pressed on the brakes as fast as we could. The back of the bikes had completely lifted off the ground. The man in the car was scared for our lives. And out of nowhere, we both landed without falling. We said that that was a warning, and we did not declare a winner. So we were both scared out of our minds and went back to the house. So all the children followed.

DC thought it would be a good idea to lock uncle Wartholomew in the basement. I was there with him, but I did not touch anything. DC immediately ran to my mother and told her that I locked my uncle in the basement. That beautiful woman called for me. I went to see what was going on. She took a belt and began whooping me from head to toe. While she was whooping me, she was telling me that I should have never locked my uncle in the basement. I turned toward her face with tears big as turtles, and I said, "Mom, DC did it, and I watched." She stopped whooping me and told me that I should have never watched and to get out of her face. DC was upset with me, so he refused to speak to me. I then turned toward the TV and began watching the best musical *Grease*.

While I was watching the movie, DC had cut on the stove. He took a medal fork and held it on the fire for a few minutes. Then he ran to me with that fork in his hand. He scared me, so I turned around. Once I turned around, he placed the fork on my left arm. I screamed like I had just seen a ghost. Mom yelled at me. He laughed and said I didn't mean to. If there was such a thing as a fourth-degree burn, I would have had it. To this day, I still have that burn mark.

Time, days, and weeks had passed. I felt a sense of no purpose. I had no drive, no motivation, no family that I felt loved me, and no friends that I could call. Attempt 1, this day, I had the house to myself. I had woken up late and wasn't quite sure where everyone had gone. I was hungry without an appetite. I was in pain, but I couldn't feel it. And I was pale but fully nourished. I walked back and forth from the kitchen to the living room pasting. Thoughts scrambled my brain. My heart began to race. I asked the Lord to take me home. I told him that I wanted to die and wasn't afraid. So I went to the kitchen and found the sharpest knife. I put the knife to my heart and told HIM if he has a purpose for me going through all this pain, then save me. I wanted a quick death, so with two hands on the knife and a lot of pressure, I took a deep breath and began to force the knife to my heart. I got one inch away from my heart, and to my surprise, out of nowhere, my sister came up the stairs. She saved me, or maybe I should say he saved me.

> Trust in the LORD with all your heart and lean not on your own understanding. (Proverbs 3:5 NIV)

CHAPTER 6

The Known and the Unknown

Woe to my precious, my sweet family. Oh my, what did you do? You must have done something that was distasteful in the eyes of the Lord. You must have opened doors and different ports. You must have committed the ultimate sin, blasphemy, because we thought we were cursed.

Things were hard for me mainly because I could not separate dreams from reality. They were vivid dreams with remarkable details to the point where I knew exactly where I was going to go and who I was going to meet. But they went farther than the eye could see. I would see something I called to be a "death line" occasionally. But in reality, it was the spirit that governed them. But even further than that, the Lord allowed my eyes to witness the supernatural intertwined with nature.

The home that we lived in was an old nursery. We lived upstairs in the two-bedroom home, and my grandparents lived downstairs in the three-bedroom home. One night, my grandparents were hosting dinner, so all the children were upstairs, watching one of our favorite movies, which was a musical. My grandparents had eleven children, so they needed a table to fit that many children. It was a cherrywood table that was extremely wide. My mother was heavy into African art. She had a nude African woman holding a cup the same size as her body. On that day, the African statue sat on the cherry wood table and was pushed all the way back to the wall. The table was pushed as far back toward the wall as possible, leaving no room, just a wall. My cat was in my lap, and all the adults were downstairs. All the children sat in the living room. We all heard a screeching noise. So we looked at each other with a spooked look. Then the screeching got louder and louder. It waited until it had all our attention. There the statue stood in the midair away from the table, giving us enough time to react. Then out of nowhere, it slammed against the floor, breaking into a million pieces. We had scattered like roaches when the light hit them. We all ran downstairs yelling, screaming, and telling the adults what happened. They just laughed.

That house should have been called "the Glass House." The only difference was that it wasn't missing the thirteenth ghost. One day, my grandmother and I were the only two in the house. So we decided that day that we would make some glass and paint it. The kiln was in the basement, along with the molds. Our basement was huge. It had rooms inside of rooms. It was so big that a full-size family could live down there comfortably. As my grandmother and I walked down the stairs, the temperature dropped, and we began to shiver. Once we entered the basement, we took a sharped left. We entered the room, and the mold that Grandma was looking for was on the other side of the room. I stood by the door, and Grandma began to walk over there.

She began speaking, and I couldn't hear her. So I raised my voice because there was quite some distance between us. She said, "Why are you raising your voice?"

I said to Grandma, "I'm way over here!"

She turned around and said, "You were standing directly next to me."

I said, "No, ma'am. I have been standing right here since we came down here." Her eyes got really big, and she looked past me. She said, "I need you to come to me as quickly as possible and do not look behind you." In a scared voice, I said okay. She then kneeled down to me and said, "There is something by the door, and it's pointing to you. It can't have you. Now we have to go back through those doors, but it's okay, I got you. I need you to close your eyes and let me guide you." But curious as a cat, I looked. There it stood tall as the ceiling, black shadowy, a hat from the '60s, no face, mysterious, and captivating. It was like looking into a dark hole all while being sucked into it. As we went up the stairs, it was like it was calling to me without a voice.

As time went on, things began to appear as though it was the norm. Children may be from the corn, animals, not so bad ones, evil ones, and ones that just wanted you to listen. One day, I told my dad's mother, my granny. Granny had six children. I only knew four of the children: my dad, my aunt Moornie, my uncle Brice, and my aunt China. Granny was a wise woman. She told me, "Never to talk to them because once you begin to talk to them, you become more susceptible to them. And once you become more susceptible to them, you begin to play with fire because we are more spiritual beings than human beings. There are angels, and there are demons. And what you are describing does not sound like any angel that I have read about."

Granny was a righteous woman. She lived for God and by God. Her purpose was to make sure my brother, sister, and I had a foundation built so that we wouldn't stray. She was an angel. Everything she said was golden. So I listened to her. Heaven was missing one angel until her purpose was fulfilled. I would not talk to them, but they did everything possible to get my attention. I remember waking up with scratches on my arms and legs. I remember hearing screams. I remember things saying I was not welcome in that home. I remember something trying to get rid of me.

> For no prophecy was ever produced by the will of man, but men spoke from God as they were carried along by the Holy Spirit. (2 Peter 1:21 ESV)

Once I reached middle school, my school was no longer in my backyard; it was about three blocks away from me going in the opposite direction. I would walk to school with my best friend. Her name was Sophia. Sophia lived one block away from me going toward the school on Chalmers. She was pretty sweet, a tad bit shy, goofy, and she hung out with me never to question why. One day, she met me halfway. As we were walking, this dog came from the opposite direction, toward us. It was running as though it was about to attack. The foam increased by its mouth. The growl got louder. It felt like the ground was shaking. Not to mention, it was white pit bull. My friend was about to start running. Closer and closer it came to us, so fast like the wind was bringing it to us. She was shaking. I told her it was okay. And he did not want to harm us. He got to us, and in midair, he jumped right into my arms and licked my whole face. I took that as a sign that that day was going to be great. My friend was really weirded out. She said, "How did you know it wouldn't bite you? Why weren't you scared?" I said, "I don't know." I could feel peace when he was running toward me.

As the school day went on, things were regular. My class was my homeroom teacher who hated me. I think I reminded her of someone. She would always make comments on how dumb I was. It didn't bother me because the things she said, I had already heard before. My math teacher was Mrs. Magy. Boy, was she amazing! She was the teacher who loved me like I was her child. She never spoke bad to me. She told me that I was beautiful. And on some days, she'd hug me out of nowhere. She talked to me like I was a human. She understood that math was not my strong suit, so she taught me in ways that I would understand it. She used the one thing that I loved to help me understand math. She used food. I could go on for chapters about how that woman was an angel to me. My science teacher was amazing. When she walked into the room, it lit up behind her. My reading teacher was a pain in my hip. She would always call on me to read knowing that I struggled with reading. Words would often jump around when I look at them. Often I would see additional letters added to a word. And to top it off, I couldn't remember what I had just learned. So I struggled when it came to speaking. I didn't know then, but I know now that I was dyslexic. My homeroom teacher would always tell me that she knew something. It would go like this; I would be spacing off, and she would yell at me, calling me by my first name, saying, "If you don't do some work. I KNOW SOMETHING." I never truly understood what that meant. I just took it as my warning.

That day, I went to lunch. I sat with my friend, and she had friends, so we all sat together. One girl was not my enemy, but it was unknown that she was not my friend. She was the type of person that talked about everybody. And once she opened her mouth, everyone laughed. You did not want to be on her bad side because she would make you feel smaller than small. Her name was Rochelle. We ate our lunch. And every word that came out of her mouth was distasteful. She hit my leg to see if I was in agreement with her. The first time, I did not say anything. Then something weird began to happen. I began to see the deathlike thing entering her body. She hit me again, and I grabbed her hand. And I told her if she doesn't stop talking about people, her death line would increase. And soon it will consume her whole body. The voice that was speaking through me was deep and direct. She looked at me as though she felt that voice that is a feeling. Or maybe I scared her. From that point on, she would not talk about people around me. And to my surprise, she did not talk about me anymore.

> Now concerning spiritual gifts, brothers, I do not want you to be uninformed. You know that when you were pagans you were led astray to mute idols, however you were led. Therefore I want you to understand that no one speaking in the Spirit of God ever says "Jesus is accursed!" and no one can say "Jesus is Lord" except in the Holy Spirit. Now there are varieties of gifts, but the same Spirit; and there are varieties of service, but the same Lord. (1 Corinthians 12:1-3 NIV)

CHAPTER 7

IT

The summers in Detroit were beautiful. The temperatures were not hot. The wind was perfect. The grass was freshly cut. So the scent was mesmerizing. Birds chirped every morning and periodically throughout the day. Those days and times were of no factor. Days often mashed its way into nights running into each other.

For more than one reason, I felt invisible, and I absolutely hated being home. I only spoke to a few people at school, which kept me from going crazy. Additionally, I was a part of after-school programs, and I played sports. In the after-school programs, I found peace because I no longer had to be Britteny. I could be the girl who had a bright smile or the smart girl. Anything besides who I actually was was okay with me. With sports, I played mental sports and physical sports. I played academic games. I ran track. I played golf. I played tennis and softball. Needless to say, the only thing that I was really good at was academic games. As long as I wasn't in a place where people were going to judge me, going to be mean just because the sky is blue, and wasn't going to try to fight me, I was content.

Happiness was something that I craved. Peace of mind was something I dreamed of. Love was something I admired. Torment was something I received. And pain was something that almost drowned me. For years, I associated pain with anger. Those days, I was a ticking time bomb. I would hold it all in until everyone in my pathway was burning from the flames that I was throwing.

One day, while I was in middle school, these girls who knew me from elementary decided that they were going to jump me. They threatened me every day and told me that if they caught me by myself that they would beat me to a point of unrecognition. In the hallways, they'd bump me. At lunch, they stared me down. And in class, every time I opened my mouth, they'd call me dumb, stupid, the girl who couldn't read, four eyes, Labrador retriever (which was a play on my last name). The threats and bullying lasted for the duration of my middle school.

One day, my best friend at the time, Trina Wobbles, told me she was not going to make it to school. I hung out in a pack, so to speak. It was Trina Wobbles who was popular, Trina Razor (they had the same first name) who was crazy so people didn't step out of line with her, and me who was smart. So I told her if she won't be in school, then I can't be in school because they will literally end it for me. She said, "Okay, I will talk to my mom because it is national skip day." I said okay. That day, I walked by the school, and people from my class waved and shouted my name. She had told me to come to her house. So that day, for the first time, I skipped school. It was kinda cool, I thought. Trina's mom cooked us breakfast. See, Trina had come from a big family. I want to say that she had thirteen siblings. She was my best friend because she knew how to live her life and did not care who judged and was given the freedom to do as she pleased. She was a beauty. We talked and talked, and sang and danced and laughed. We had so much fun! She did my makeup and hair. She made me feel wanted. And that's all I ever wanted.

So after a few hours of hanging at her house, her older sisters wanted to go to the gas station. So myself and four of her sisters began to walk to the store. As we were walking, I looked up and saw my sister, the Boss, and Jessica. So I did my best to hide behind Trina. Well, I later found out that my hide-and-go-seek skills were trash because everybody saw me. We continued walking, and as we were about to walk into the gas station, I saw my brother coming out of the gas station. He winked at me, so I took it as a sign that he would not tell Mommy. Then we walked into the gas station, and I saw my Aunt Bea who resembled Aunt Lea and her daughter Ieasha. Oh my goodness, I was dying in the inside. I thought for sure that the beautiful woman was going to kill me. "So why not enjoy my final moments of life?"

We got what we needed from the store, and her sister's decided that we should go over BaDambsy's house. He lived five minutes away from the store by foot. My Spidey senses began to tingle. The voice that was the filling began screaming at me. I began to shake. Trina said, "What's wrong?"

I said, "I don't think we should go over there."

She said, "I will be all right because you are with me." BaDambsy was a major drug dealer, killer, and woman abuser. He made quite a track record for himself so much so that he was on the Feds' radar. I knew that my great-grandmother lived right across the street. So while we were walking, I switched coats with Trina so that my family would not recognize me. We entered the house. Once we got in, they locked the doors from inside with a key. I had thought that was a tad bit strange. So I asked, "Why did you lock us in?"

One of the guys that was at the house said, "Because female dogs don't leave." Then he began to laugh. Something said, "Run." So they put on so inappropriate videos and began to let natural herbs fill the air. My heart began to race. Sweat began to run down my face. Then out of nowhere, the doorbell rang. It was my family. They told him to let me out of the house. He told them that I was not in the house. Wolf tickets and treats began to fill the air. What I forgot to mention was that yes, he was a drug dealer, but my family was equivalent to the mafia. So I told my friend that I was going to jump out the bathroom window if it's open or find another way to leave before it's too late. She grabbed my hand and told me it was going to be okay and to quietly exit because if they found me trying to escape, the punishment would be much worse. So I told them that I needed to go to the restroom for woman issues.

Once I got to the restroom, by the grace of God, the window was open. I jumped out the window and climbed a fence. Once I was completely out of harm's way, once I landed on the other side of the fence, I knew that he was still watching me. A pastor came up to me because I had jumped a fence, and that was a fence to his church. He said, "Does your parents know where you are?"

I said, "Yes."

He said, "Why did you jump the fence?"

"Because they locked me in the house."

"How long were you there?"

"A few hours."

"Go home."

So I said okay. There was only one problem with that scenario. It was noon, and I didn't get out of school until 3:30 p.m. So I went inside of this blue and white furniture store and sat there for about an hour. When a woman asked me what was I doing, I told her I was waiting on my mom to pick me up. She said, "What's your mom's number so I can call her?" I looked at her with fear in my eyes and grabbed my backpack and began to walk down a street called Charlmers. The next street over was my street, Lakewood. As I was walking, I looked in the alley leading to my street. There was a man there, and for a moment, my spirit eyes were opened. I could see the thing that trapped him. He had a ferocious spirit that was hungry for me. I kept walking because he was on the other street. At every ally, he was there, so I started running. He started running. I ran into my old elementary BFF's house. And I stayed there until about 3:35 p.m. I began to turn the corner and went home. Lo and behold, the creep was waiting on me. He ran up to me and put a knife to my neck and asked me a question that I didn't understand, so I said, "The muffin man lives on Drury Lane."

He said, "What is it, Red?"

I said, "Bloody." He then slowly put the knife down, and I never saw him again. But when I got home, what was waiting on me was worse. Without any questions, I was beaten so much so that I began to bleed. I guess it did get bloody. But my mom made a deal with me. She said that if she talked to the teacher and the teacher said I was in school, she'll tell the family that it was a misunderstanding. But if she confirms that I was skipping school, she is going to let the whole family have a taste of me. So the next day, I went to school and begged my teacher to vouch for me. He said everyone was looking for me, even my dad. He also told me that he was very disappointed in me, and he asked why. So I told him everything. He told her that I am a straight-A student who has never been in trouble, so if something did happen, then it was for a reason. He grabbed that beautiful woman's arm and said, "Please go easy on her. I can assure you that she has learned her lesson. She's a good girl." So we got home, and the family was waiting all ready to attack me. But knowing what she knew, she spared me and told the family that I was in school. Later, I found out that it was my brother who called the school looking for me after he saw me. Oh, I FORGOT to mention, that summer, a random guy pulled a gun on me because I wouldn't give him my number. Boy! That was PTSD in a nutshell.

A little bit of time had passed. It was so vibrant, so pulsating, that everyone who came to our house knew I didn't belong. My aunt Web had two children, Tammy and Shontelle. Tammy was bright, brilliant, bodacious, bad, and bleak. She was something like a kaleidoscope. How you viewed her depends on how you saw her. I saw a complex beauty. So one summer, my cousin Shontelle, who was the oldest of the two, asked the Boss if she wanted to go to a theme park called Cedar Point. She jumped for joy. So they left for the day. The question that flooded my thoughts was, *Why didn't she ask me?* But when they returned, she had brought me a jogging suit, for I loved sports, so I forgave her. A few weeks later, we were on summer break. Shontelle asked me if I wanted to get away. Without hesitation, I said YES. For I thought, *Finally. He was more than smiling down on me, and he was removing me from these crazy people too.* To my surprise, my mother said I could go. This was a shock because she had never let me fly, for she always kept me under her wings.

My cousin Shontelle has two children. Her children are Dyshown and Kebri. Dyshown, he is the oldest of the two, and Kebri, she is the baby girl. Shontelle lived in Southfield. She had an apartment with her boyfriend of about seven years at that time. My cousin made me feel so pretty. She would do my hair and let me wear some of her clothing. Sometimes she would let me invite one of my friends over. There was a different type of beauty that surrounded her. She looked like she was seventeen. She had dimples deeper than deep with beautiful teeth. To add to that, she was like sour-patch kids. First, she was sour, and then she was sweet. For anyone who would take me away from those people was beautiful to me.

As time went on, I started to gain a little confidence. The clothing that she let me wear began to hug my body. She would sometimes put makeup on my eyes, bringing out the light brown color of my eyes. For a split second, I was happy. During that time, I would often sit outside and let her children play at the apartment playground. I would let the sun consume me and get lost in it. One day, a guy named James came to the park. He was about six feet four inches. His hair was smooth as a baby's butt. His smile was gorgeous. His hands were huge. He was tall, dark, and handsome. And he was nice to me. He said, "Hey, beautiful."

I smiled and said, "Hi, sir." He laughed, and we began to talk. Before I knew it, I had a boyfriend who was eighteen years old. And by the way, did I mention that I was thirteen? We talked about everything. He told me his parents abandoned him, and for the past few years, it was just him and his sister. He was raising her. He would buy me lunch, and every day we would eat together. He would hold my hand and had no problem showing me to his friends. He was so beautiful to me. I would then get up every morning smiling, knowing he would be waiting on me.

One day, we both had on rose-colored glasses. He began hugging and kissing all over my body. I liked it because no one had ever shown me this type of attention before. He picked me up and began taking off my clothing. I stopped him and said, "What are you doing?" He then placed my hand on his private area. I freaked out because I had never felt anyone's body parts before. And he said, "I want you."

I said, "You have me."

He said, "No, I want you," in a strange voice.

I then stepped back and said, "I am a virgin."

Persistent as he was, he grabbed my hand and said, "Let me be your first," while bringing me closer to his body. My eyes then filled with water, and I removed his hands from me. I said, "No, I can no longer see you. This is the end." I then took my fingers, kissed them, and placed them on his forehead. His eyes filled with water as I walked away.

A few days later, his friend was talking to my cousin Shontelle. He told her that I was talking to his friend. I then told him in front of her that it didn't work out. He said, "James is really crazy about you. You should give him another chance." I smiled and walked away. I would continue with my routine, take the kids to the playground, and let the sun watch me as time elapsed. One day, as I sat on the bench, my mind was on him so much that I did not notice the playground was full of his friends, family, and him. When I came to the realization, I jumped. They certainly startled me. His sister came to me and said, "Why did you hurt my brother?" She began banging her hands against her fist. Then some other girl whom I hadn't met until that moment began to call me all sorts of female dogs. A crowd of people crowded around me. I looked at the children. And it must have been an angel in the mist because my thoughts were to keep playing, and once the crowd dies down some, go to the apartment and lock the doors. And they did just that. I moved further away from the playground, giving the children time to run. Once they got in the building, I took off running. For I had never gotten into a real fight before. I had a good distance from the crowd. So I ran up three flights of stairs and hid in one of the laundry rooms. I hid behind one of the dryers. I hid for about two hours.

While I was hiding, about three hundred more people were added to the crowd. There were so many people that you would have thought they were rioting. I looked out the window of the laundry room and saw *Fox News* outside. The story had gotten so twisted up that by the time it got back to me, the rumor was that I had slept with his friend and had cut him with a knife. He had scouts on every floor. As I was leaving the laundry room, I saw that friend that was talking to my cousin. He had a strange look on his face. Then out of nowhere, he began running toward me. I saw that spirit that was over him, and I ran to the apartment like my life depended on it. All I could hear was "THERE SHE GO, GET HER! Run, run, run." Maybe this was the purpose of those sports.

I arrived at my cousin's apartment sweating, crying, and shaking. She was confused and angry. She then yelled at me saying, "What did you do? WHAT DID YOU DO?" She realized that I was terrified. She then calmed her nerves and said, "I need you to start from the beginning. What happened?" So I told her everything. And she hugged me and said, "I thought you were going to tell me something else." They began to bang on the door almost as though they were going to tear it down. So she grabbed a metal bat and opened the door. I didn't mention that she was borderline crazy. She hit everyone that was in the front and dared them to come closer. The crowd started backing up. She cursed them out, and it was something vicious. Then she told me to come out of the apartment. She said, "Do y'all not realize that she is thirteen years old and he is eighteen? If anything, I could call the cops, and all of y'all would be arrested." Then she pointed him out and called him a coward.

Someone in the crowd said, "Let the dogs loose."

She said in a loud and deep voice, "Get the gun." The crowd began to leave because they found out how old I was. She called my other older cousins in disbelief. They came over. And they could not believe it either that these people tried to harm me over a guy that was five years older than me whom I had NO intercourse with and whom I only dated for a month.

Beautiful as he was, shining down on me, I awoke. Over the next few days, I stayed in the house to make sure things were dead. My cousin worked nights. She was a cleaning woman. The apartment hadn't been the cleanest, so I wanted to surprise her. I cleaned the whole apartment, even the kids' room. Afterward, the kids were hungry, and my tummy began to talk as well. There was absolutely NO food. There was no lunch meat. There was no bread. There was no peanut butter. There were no noodles. There wasn't even any juice to get full off of. Hours had gone by, and it felt like my stomach was eating itself. I was so hungry that I wanted to go outside and beg for money so that we could eat. I was just about to give up.

But then out of nowhere, my baby cousin Dyshown yelled and said, "I found some food." Kebri and I ran to him. He had found some mashed potatoes in the box hidden under the counter. He put water, butter, salt, and pepper in it; and he let it cook for thirty minutes. When it was finished, he fixed Kebri and I a plate. It was the best mashed potatoes I had ever had. They were so good that I went to the bathroom and began to cry. I was so happy to have eaten something, and that something was really good. I cleaned up the mess, and by that time, it was time for the children to go to bed. I knew that the time for my cousin Shontelle to come home was near. So I re-vacuumed the floor, and I lit candles. (For she would be so proud and so happy when she comes home is what I thought.)

Time had passed, and I began to go into a world I only knew as "dreamland." This dream scared me. Something really bad had happened. Her boyfriend had made a sexual gesture toward me. So I told her, and in the dream, she said, "I don't believe you. You are a liar, and GET OUT." All those feelings of distrust, of loneliness, and sadness consumed me. Instantly, I WOKE UP. The door slammed open. Kebri got up to see her mommy. I smiled because I knew she was going to be proud of me. To my surprise, it wasn't her. It was her boyfriend. His eyes and teeth were glowing green. I could see his death line. The spirit of perversion was over him. He immediately came over to me and began kissing me. I was so scared that I could not move. He began to pull his pants down. I looked past him, and my baby cousin Kebri was there. So I covered my face. Tears rolled down my head. He then put his man piece in me. For what seemed like hours, he had his way with me. When I woke up, blood was everywhere. I thought I had to be dreaming. I told myself that I was dreaming. My cousin Shontelle had yet to come home. And there was blood all over her couch. I thought I better clean this up because she will surely kick me out if I had bled on her couch. So I cleaned it up. I then got in the shower, and my vagina began to pulsate. At this point, I was still in disbelief. I cleaned myself and put on my clothes. I went to the kitchen because an unusual hunger came over me. Soon as I stepped in the kitchen, he was in there, and it hit me like a sucker punch in the left eye that it was not a dream. He then saw the look that was on my face and saw me shaking. He said, "I will kill you if you tell anyone."

"Run, run, run as fast as you can. You can't catch me. I'm the gingerbread man." Scared as I was, I ran until I could not run anymore. I disappeared for hours. And I found myself on the roof of the apartment complex. There was a weird door. *Attempt 2*, I opened the door. The sun gazed at me. The wind blew my body, and whispers of the Lord comforted me. The wind guided me to the edge of the building. There I sat. For my thoughts were confused. I thought, *I must die because I have to tell someone. Maybe I could tell my cousin.* Then I remembered she wouldn't believe me because that's what the vision showed me. Then I thought, *I could tell my sister.* But I remembered she would probably laugh at me. Next, I thought about my mother. But then I remember that my mother had not taken up for me thus far, so why would she do it now? Finally, I thought I could tell my friend. But then she would probably tell the principal. So at that point, I realized that I had no one to tell. I began getting closer to the edge, so close that my butt cheeks were hanging off the edge. At this point, I had made it up in my mind that I must die. With no fear I was about to die, I wanted death to find me. Then out of nowhere, that voice that was a feeling came over me and told me to stop! He showed me in a vision that he would not let me die from this twelve-story fall. But I would be paralyzed for life. Unable to speak, unable to walk, unable to marry or have children, and most importantly, my mother would not recognize me. I began to cry out loud, and a wind PUSHED ME BACK! At that moment, he said, "**You are not alone, and nor have you ever been.**" For hours, it felt like someone was holding me and crying with me. I did not tell anyone. But I was so messed up that I would have rather stayed in a small apartment with a man who raped me then have went home to my mother who did not want me.

> The Lord tests the righteous, but his soul
> hates the wicked and the one who loves violence.
> (Psalm 11:5 ESV)

It was time for me to go home. But because I didn't want to feel that pain, my young mind thought, *If I must live, then I will live as a boy. For no one would ever harm a boy.* So I stopped caring about my hair. I washed up maybe twice a week. Because boys were always stinky, so I had assumed that that's what they did. I played basketball with the guys because they seemed to like it. I found myself wanting to hump all my cousins and them wanting to hump me. It was like I smelled of estrogen, dopamine, and norepinephrine 24-7 because men, women, boys, and girls all wanted a piece of me. In the midst of it all, my feelings toward people became numb. I blamed myself for trying to have some confidence. I blamed my mother for allowing me to go away and not even noticing that I had not returned. I blamed my cousin's boyfriend for the drugs he was on. I shut the world out, for I refused to talk to anyone. Then I went into a box that was deeply compressed to the point where I became heavily depressed. For I was broken permanently is what I thought.

> But the Lord said to Samuel, "Do not look on his appearance or on the height of his stature, because I have rejected him. For the Lord sees not as man sees: man looks on the outward appearance, but the Lord looks on the heart."
> (1 Samuel 16:7 ESV)

Years had passed, and I thought that I was invincible. So I really believed that I was invincible. Things were still the same at the house. At school, people still were mean to me. They still pushed me around, and they still said bad things about me. Everywhere I went and everybody I came in contact with still treated me like I was the redheaded stepchild. The irony in that is that I was born with red hair. I hadn't heard that voice that was a feeling in a while, so I thought it would be a good idea to tempt him.

Attempt 3, I knew that I was gifted, but I didn't understand it. I was walking home from school one day, and to get home, I had to cross a major street. We had no crossing guards or even a light to slow the traffic. The speed limit was thirty miles per hour, but the flow of traffic was about seventy-five miles per hour. To cross the street, we had to wait until there was no traffic, then run across. This day,

I did not want to die, but I wanted to hear from the voice that was a feeling; and I thought the only way to hear from him was in death or near death. So I waited to see if I could see someone driving who wasn't paying attention. I began crossing the street. Cars flew by me. The middle of the street was near. I looked behind me and the cars were going so fast the wind from the cars blew my body. I looked in front of me, and the same thing happened. My heart began to race. My sweat glands began to open, and my body began to freeze. I looked up, and there was this car speeding and not paying attention. I began to feel as though it was the end for me. The wind pushed me so close to the car that my nose had almost touched the car. At that moment, in the middle of the street, the Lord spoke directly to me. He said, **"Do not tempt the Lord."** Those words felt like fire had hit my heart. When I finally made it across the street, I began to cry out to the Lord saying, "I did not want to die. I just wanted to hear from you. You are the only one who has ever comforted me." In that moment, it felt like all my peace, that thing that I had felt watching over me my whole life, it felt like it was leaving me. Confusing as it sounds, that's what it was.

> And God spoke all these words, saying, "I am the Lord your God, who brought you out of the land of Egypt, out of the house of slavery. "You shall have no other gods before me. "You shall not make for yourself a carved image, or any likeness of anything that is in heaven above, or that is in the earth beneath, or that is in the water under the earth. You shall not bow down to them or serve them, for I the Lord your God am a jealous God, visiting the iniquity of the fathers on the children to the third and the fourth generation of those who hate me. (Exodus 20:1–2 ESV)

Over the next months, he did not smile down on me. I thought for sure he had abandoned me. So I stayed to myself because I did not want to taint anyone else. Sometimes, I would test the waters to see if maybe he was still watching me. I thought that because it felt like he abandoned me, that the gifts that he bestowed on me would leave too. Sometimes, I would just touch people who were mistreating me, and I would be able to see the pain that would follow them. Often I would tell them about it, and that did not end well. They would call me all types of names running from A to Z. Then in the midst of that, I became consumed with telling people about their future. Their pain excited me and gave me motivation. I was becoming someone else. No wait, I was becoming something else. Pain from my family no longer hurt. Pain from school no longer hurt, and pain from boys no longer hurt.

At school, there was this girl named Raina Benery. She was sometimes a friend. Sometimes she was my friend, and other times she was not. This relationship was okay with me and okay with her. She'd often call me a free spirit. I did not know what it meant, so it did not bother me. She said that it was something in me that was really peaceful and she didn't mind me because I did not judge people, that sometimes relationships begin to disappear. She began talking to me more and more.

One day, she shared with me that she was Wiccan. I asked her what it meant to be Wiccan. She said it means to do magic. This intrigued me because I hadn't met anyone who could do real magic. She said, "Do you want to learn?"

I said, "Well, I am not sure because I am Christian." She then began to tell me things about the Bible that I did not know.

She said, "Did you know that God and Jesus are the same person?" (This blew my mind.)

I said, "No, that's not right. My granny said that we must believe in the Father, the Son, and the Holy Spirit, which means that they are three people."

She said, "If you think I am lying, go and ask your granny. And if you find that I am telling you the truth, will you try Wicca?"

I said, "I guess."

But my granny would never lie to me. She lives for God. My brother, sister, and myself saw our granny on weekends because we went to church every Sunday. On this particular day, I asked her, "Granny, is God and Jesus the same person?"

My granny said yes. And she began explaining, but I could not hear what she was saying because I kept thinking that Raina was right. I didn't know that there are levels of Christianity. For I was a babe. From that, I became Wiccan. I thought I could get in it to get her out of it. I did not no know that I was playing with fire. And that a bruda viper had just spit some venom. I did not know that I was opening ports. I did not know that my gifts could be used for evil. And I did not know that I was Raina Benery's pawn. Better yet, I did not know that I was doing the will of IT', and moving further away from HIM.

Thoughts: *What do I do if I want to be near him? What do I do if I want to feel him? Voice that is a feeling, please don't leave. Wait, what do I believe?*

Tomorrow was like my today. He was full of love. He is currently my longest friend. I met him in the second grade. Tomorrow went to elementary, middle school, and high school with me. He was always the most popular kid. Women went crazy over him, and every guy wanted to fight him. He was the type of person that if you pulled his card, he'd show you his hand. I brought him up because he was a big dreamer. They say you can be a dreamer but don't say in your bed. No one could confirm it, but everyone knew that I and him had a secret. The secret was that innocence was lost between us. We planned to get married; we planned to have between us four kids. Oh, and by the way, he was my neighbor. He was a special friend because when my world came crashing down every time, he'd be there to pick me up. The crazy thing about him is that twenty years later, he still held on to that dream.

A friend loves at all times, and a brother is
born for adversity. (Proverbs 17:17)

So Saul died for his breach of faith. He
broke faith with the Lord in that he did not keep
the command of the Lord, and also consulted

a medium, seeking guidance. He did not seek guidance from the Lord. Therefore the Lord put him to death and turned the kingdom over to David the son of Jesse. (1 Chronicles 10:13-14 ESV)

No temptation has overtaken you that is not common to man. God is faithful, and he will not let you be tempted beyond your ability, but with the temptation he will also provide the way of escape, that you may be able to endure it. (1 Corinthians 10:13)

C HAPTER 8

The Dreams/Visions

But a child is what I was, with childlike thoughts and childlike understanding. With dreams and visions that were as powerful as the cannon. Some came as a child and as an adult. I didn't tell them all, just the ones that stood out.

One night, I remember feeling a cold that I could not shake. I remember feeling scared to the point that if I moved, IT would have got me. I remember thinking that I must be the only person in the world seeing this; and I knew, without a shadow of a doubt, that I was not, nor am I crazy. I thought I was asleep, but if I were asleep, why was it that everything was exactly the same? My sister was still next to me asleep. My brother was still on the top bunk bed asleep, and I was lying in the bed fully aware of everything. Before I knew it, I could not move a single muscle in my body. The light flickered in the bathroom, which was right across our room. Then out of nowhere, that tall black shadow thing came into the room. It stood over me, sucking the life out of me. I could see me leaving my body. And then out of nowhere, my memories of that night began to fade. When I woke up, I could not breathe. I could not catch my breath. My heart was racing, and I was sweating so bad that you would have thought that I had just got out of the swimming pool. The time was 3:00 a.m. I ran to my mother's room to tell her what had just happened. And for the first time, she had listened. She asked me was I okay to go back to bed or did I need her to stay up for me. Of course,

38

I said, stay up. But midway through me explaining to her what had just happened, she fell asleep. I looked at her, and I could see the tiredness. But I could also see that she was trying. I let her go to bed, and I said, "If my mother is tired, how would she be able go to work? If she cannot work, how would we be able to eat? And if we cannot eat, we will surely die." Did I mention that I was an overthinker, and some people would call it to be catastrophizing?

> When I was a child, I spoke like a child,
> I thought like a child, I reasoned like a child.
> When I became a man, I gave up childish ways.
> (1 Corinthians 13:11 ESV)

Every day for years, I would wake up at 3:00 a.m. And every day I would have a crazy experience. This went on for years upon years.

Time and time again, I would have a dream that I was running from something or dying. One night, I fell into a deep sleep. In the dream, I was on the city bus going somewhere. Out of nowhere, time stopped. The bus stop moving. The people on the bus stopped talking and moving. As I said, everything stopped. I looked around, and there the bus had three exits. When I realized the bus had three exits, out of nowhere, three guys appeared by the exit. Their eyes were red as wine, and their heads were like owls. They turned 360 degrees. They looked at me and smiled. I then jumped out of the bus window and began to run. For a moment, I thought I was safe, so I stopped running. The crowds of people in the streets began to get louder and larger. I could not see the three things that were after me. Then I took a deep breath, and in that moment, they caught me. They held my body down and began to rip off my shirt. In the dream, I closed my eyes screaming, "NOT AGAIN." To my surprise, they did not do what I thought they were going to do. Instead, they marked me. They burned a cross in the center of my chest. I woke up in a fright. I could smell sulfur. My chest was hurting, and where they marked me in the dream, it was extremely red. Wait. Wasn't I asleep? Why am I red? For I thought, *Why did the beast mark me? Am I doomed for hell? Maybe that's why the voice that was a feeling left.*

Maybe he already knew. Was I trapped in a mental cell or under a spell? And was this the scent of hell this here I smell?

Thoughts: *Why was I hunted by my dreams? Why was I haunted by those things? Lord, I know that I am not evil. I want nothing but the best for people. I want to help them. I can help them especially with my gifts. I want to see them succeed and be the best that they can be. Oh, Lord, why am I hunted? Why am I cursed? What does IT need from me? Or just maybe, the Lord did not leave me. Maybe this was a test. Maybe he was preparing me for life's next steps.*

> For I know the plans I have for you, declares the Lord, plans for welfare and not for evil, to give you a future and a hope. Then you will call upon me and come and pray to me, and I will hear you. You will seek me and find me, when you seek me with all your heart. (Jeremiah 29:11–13 ESV)

I remember one night, I had a dream that I was going to meet these two guys who not only looked very similar but had similar last names. In the dream, I could smell sweat and feel unbearable heat. I did not know who these guys were or when I was going to meet them. Well, to my surprise, five years later, I joined the Army; and during physical training and schooling in South Carolina, I met the two guys. The problem that I ran into is that I had four months to introduce myself to them and talk to them. **But the story of my life is that I was too scared**. One of the guys was loud, outgoing, and made a lot of sexual gestures. And the other looked really mean. So time had passed, and we were at three and a half months. Once we got to the fourth month, we went off unto the real Army is what they said. I said hello to the one who looked really mean. And that sparked a great conversation. He was actually really nice! So I told him the dream, and he said, "Why didn't you find me earlier? We could have possibly been really good friends." This bothered me because friends was something that I craved. Then the last day came around, and I said, "Okay, one down and one to go." We all were happy that we made it, so I mustered up some strength. And I fixed my lips to speak to the other guy. But just as I was about to speak to him, he began talking about me out loud to everyone. He called me stupid because of an earlier public statement that I had made and ugly because of the "birth control" glasses that I had to wear. All at once, those past feelings came over me, and I froze. If the test was given to me that day, I would have surely failed it. I never got another chance to speak to him.

But that's too far in the future. Let's get back to the dreams and visions. I started telling older people about some of the things I was dreaming about. Some prayed over me, some told me to pray, and others told me to write it down. In my latter years, someone told me that God entrusts us with his work, and sometimes he gives us dreams and other times. Sometimes he gives us visions as key elements.

The dreams or/and visions continued. One night, in a deep sleep, I fell. But a vision is what I was shown, the Lord was finished with the earth. He took me to a place he called "the training ground." He told me to stand on his Word, and once I did that, everything/anything was possible. From that point on, it was known that my job was to train all the people. Every day the building that I was to train everyone in grew larger. The bottom floor was the training grounds, and the rest of the floors were rooms. People began to appear in their rooms. When they woke up, they still had the same bodies and face as they did on earth because the Lord said, that "we would not be able to recognize each other in our new bodies." Then out of nowhere, an angel appeared. He only spoke to one person. That person was a girl with brown eyes, with blond hair, with a square face, and who was very quiet. He told her that when she needs him to call him. It was known that he was a warrior angel, and she was to deliver a message. As the day came to an end, I began to meditate on what the Lord had told me. I began to stand on his Word, and in the moment, my body began to float. So I thought if I could float because I am standing on his Word, then I can conjure up weapons. And guess what! A weapon appeared in my hand. All night I began to test all that I could do, and to my surprise, there was nothing that I couldn't do. A day or so passed, and I told everyone that we needed to start training. Five people showed up to train. I had to explain to them that we were not on earth. We must stand on the Lord's Word, and our mission is to fight in the Army of the Lord. Some of them had questions that the Lord did not reveal to me, so I diverted the questions by showing them what we could do. We had practiced for hours it seemed like. Then we rested.

The next day or so, I told everyone that we needed to train; and on this day, everyone showed up. I had given the same message as I did the day or so prior. Now the good thing is that the lord still gave everyone free will. And some people choose not to train. Some of the people from the prior day thought that others would judge them, so they decided not to train. I had still ended up with five people who wanted to do what the Lord said to do. So it began! We closed the doors, cut off the oxygen supply, and trained harder than anyone could imagine. We thought of weapons while in the air and fought until we could not anymore. We could get tired but not hurt. So we slammed people through walls, put weapons through each, and tested all limits. WE PRACTICED!

Then it was time to rest, so we began to clean the training ground. Then out of nowhere, multitudes upon multitudes of demons appeared. They appeared in huge ships that did not need water to sail. And once they arrived, they began to take our women and children. Their leader asked for our leader, which was me. So I let them know that it was I that they were looking for, and they laughed. For they thought that a laughter would scare me and make me run. Well, they were WRONG! Everyone stood together in a stair formation. Three people would complete a row, and there were several rows. I then whispered to everyone to get ready for war. Standing right behind me was the girl that the angel had spoken to. So I whispered to her to call the angel. At that moment, the five of us that trained became warriors for God. The girl that the angel spoke to, she became a messenger, and the people that did not train became lower-classed humans in heaven. Then a girl that I went to high school with who later became my best friend named Amani Lee-zoni appeared. Out of nowhere, I woke up and said, "Thank you, Jesus, and I accept."

For several nights in the same month, Amani Lee-zoni appeared in my dreams. So through the dreams, I began to reach for her. I began to call her by name. I began praying for her in my dreams. And in the last dream that she appeared in, I said to her, "Jesus is calling you." Then she disappeared. After I woke up, I called her, but she did not answer. Little did I know that she was facing an extremely high form of depression. I would call it to be PTSD, but I am not a doctor, just a friend who went through similar things.

The Lord told me and showed me that it was up to me to get my family saved. So one night, I had this crazy dream. My family was having a party on the street Lakewood. All my family and all my friends were there. They partied like it wasn't going to be a tomorrow. Then all of a sudden, the angel of death appeared. He was about sixty feet tall, with glowing blueish greenish eyes and mouth. My family and friends were partying, but they were stuck in a trance is what it felt like. The whole time he was looking at my family, and I was looking at him. I began to get scared, shaking and hoping that it was not there to feed. Out of nowhere, it spoke to my heart and said, "Don't be afraid." It was known in the dream that if he touched you, then unfortunately, you would die. It reached out with one hand touching everyone all at once. So I began to speak life over each and every person there. I declared and decreed that "no weapon formed against them shall prosper." I said, "Get thee behind me." And things started to lighten up. He said in a stern voice, "WHAT HAVE YOU DONE?" He then began to disappear, and I woke up.

When I awoke, I prayed and prayed. And at that moment, the Lord spoke to me and said, "It is up to you to save your family."

As time went on, I prayed to the Lord to ask him, "How can I save them? What specifically do I need to do?" Over time, he said, "Spread the light." So I started sending long scriptures to everyone at 6:00 a.m. I felt proud about that because I thought that when people first wake up, that they need Jesus. (I still believe that.) But I ended up getting a lot of negative responses. This discouraged me, and I went months without sending the Word. Well, during that time, my family fell off. They began slowly killing themselves. I remember getting phones calls saying how my cousins put my uncle in the hospital or how my male cousins stabbed my female cousins or how my sister's car got stolen, it seemed like every month, or how my brother was thinking going in a different direction from his wife or how my mother wasn't happy, etc. Things went haywire for a while. And people began telling me how my messages were blessing them and how they were lost without it. So I now send short encouraging individualized messages every day around lunchtime to about fifty people.

And he said, "Hear my words: If there is a prophet among you, I the Lord make myself known to him in a vision; I speak with him in a dream. (Numbers 12:6 ESV)

A Psalm of David. The Lord is my shepherd; I shall not want. He makes me lie down in green pastures. He leads me beside still waters. He restores my soul. He leads me in paths of righteousness for his name's sake. Even though I walk through the valley of the shadow of death, I will fear no evil, for you are with me; your rod and your staff, they comfort me. You prepare a table before me in the presence of my enemies; you anoint my head with oil; my cup overflows. (Psalm 23:1–6 ESV)

CHAPTER 9

That Life

Throughout high school, I had honors classes. So in high school, I stayed with the same group of people through twelfth grade. In ninth grade biology, I met Amani Lee-zoni. She is an African woman who was beautiful to me. Her face reminded me of the Boss's face. It was completely rounded, and she was dark-skinned. She was a dark beauty. Exploring the juxtaposition between something that was beautiful and dark was intriguing. She and I were attached to each other like the white on rice. Whatever she did, I followed. Whatever I did, she followed. She was one of my first friends in high school. We were so close that my whole family knew her and her family knew me. My family took her in and loved on her. This threw me off because I had questioned if they loved me. They were patient, they were kind, they were everything that they were not with me to her. But this love wasn't fake. She loved me, she accepted me, she listened to me, and she did not judge me. What a friend she was to me. Together we were like brownies and ice cream. We just went together. "They say in life that you are lucky to at least have one good friend." Well, I must be blessed because here I stand, at thirty years old, and I have at least three. *Do your friends build you up or break you down?*

During that next year, the time had come to start looking at colleges. The scary, happy thoughts of being free and furthering our education while living our dreams was mind-blowing. I wasn't sure what I wanted to do in college or become. The only thing that I was

45

sure of was being free, hopefully with my buddy. Military recruiters came to sell us on a dream. The dream that they were selling I wasn't buying. Our class went to visit the local colleges. I remember going to visit Wayne Community College. I remember this day because it was my birthday. We had a lot of walking to do this day. Toward the end of the day, we went through the computer lab and passed Subway. The aroma filled the building, and it was as though the food was saying, "Eat me. Please eat me. I'm only $5.00 away." I only had $1.50. Oh, how my heart wanted a chocolate chip cookie. But I had to remember that I still needed $1.50 to get home on the bus at the end of the day. So the college trip was coming to a close, and they told everyone to go to the bus if you are not ordering food. With my heart almost in tears, I went to the bus. While I was walking to the bus, I heard this girl's laugh and said, "I bet her feet hurt." I forgot to mention that I had on red shiny wedges with a black and red outfit because again, it was supposed to be a special day for me. When I got on the bus, the bus driver said, "Young lady, lift your head up because you are BEAUTIFUL." I smiled and said thank you. I went toward the back of the bus where Amani was sitting. She smiled at me and leaned her head against my arm. Then out of nowhere, the football players got on the bus. They were loud and had the nerve to smell like a subway. They sat right behind Amani and me.

Then one of them started eating chocolate chip and peanut butter cookies. I couldn't contain myself. So I mustered up some courage, and I asked. I said in a tiny voice, "Excuse me, may I have a chocolate chip cookie?"

Looking directly at him, he said, "No," in a stern voice. I began to mentally beat myself up. And right before I knew it, he said, "Here's a peanut butter cookie." He then said, "What's your name?"

I said, "Britteny. What's your name?"

He said, "Nathaniel Rocket." Who knew that ten years later that Amani would be like a sister to me and Nathaniel would still be my best friend?

Throughout high school, Nathaniel Rocket stood up for me so much that the whole school thought that we were dating. They questioned it because he was like the eye candy, and I was like the black licorice that no one liked. He was five feet, ten inches, with muscles from head to toe, deep round eyes, a smile that was simply beautiful and hair that was brushed to perfection. To top it off, he had a personality where he appeared mean, but his heart was sweet. He was business minded and a straight shooter. Women literally went crazy over him, and all of them accused him of cheating on them with me. He reminded of the guy who plays Raymond off "Everybody loves Raymond." As time went on, I began to desire him. He was the first male figure that I had. He would listen to me even if I talked for hours upon hours. And if he wasn't listening, he never let me know. He began coming around my family almost every week for years which showed them how much me loved me. My love for him grew so much that I had written a piece of our wedding vows. I knew that I was going to say something about how he was **the peanut butter to my peanut butter cookies.** I accepted him for exactly who he was, and he accepted me for exactly who I was. And our love never died. For however long it takes, we will be together is what each of us thought. But of course, things don't always go in the direction you plan. For many years, we end up playing a game of *Tom and Jerry,* but eventually, that cat fall in love with mouse, and the mouse could not live without the cat. (Sometimes, you have to speak it in the atmosphere and believe it with your whole heart, and just maybe it'll come to pass.) *If you want to know a funny joke, tell God your plans.*

> Two are better than one, because they have
> a good reward for their toil. For if they fall, one
> will lift up his fellow. But woe to him who is
> alone when he falls and has not another to lift
> him up! Again, if two lie together, they keep
> warm, but how can one keep warm alone? And
> though a man might prevail against one who is
> alone, two will withstand him—a threefold cord
> is not quickly broken. (Ecclesiastes 4:9–12 ESV)

College time, YAY! This is how everyone felt. The time was near for us to go our separate ways. Each of us went to different places.

Amani went to Michigan State University. Nathaniel went to Iowa State University, and I went to Wayne State University. As happy as we were to start our new lives and escape the thing that was holding us down, we were even sadder to start out new lives without each other. This was not goodbye but simply a see you later.

My first year of college, I stayed on campus. This was a whole new life for me. There were people from every type of background. There were crazy workout facilities. The campus itself was huge. Because I had no car or license and I had to walk everywhere on campus, I would estimate that the campus was about thirty miles long and about thirty miles wide. Maybe that's a slight exaggeration. But my point is that because this was a new environment, and everything seemed to be enlarged.

The days were beyond beautiful and peaceful. Maybe because I made though, maybe that dark cloud had finally lifted from me, I now had a sense of urgency. Was I was now free?

I came up with a daily routine. I would not set an alarm to get up. I would wait until he smiled down on me, gracing me with his presence, allowing to get up. I would shower, then go down to the cafeteria, and eat what I called a loose egg. The name *loose egg* started off as a joke between the cafeteria worker and myself. It was simply sausage, ham, cheese, bell peppers, tomatoes, banana pepper, and onions grilled into my scrambled eggs. And swallowed down with a big cup of orange juice. Afterward, I would go back to my room and get dressed for the day. This was my daily for the first month or so. But then I began to get bored, and I realized that I still had no friends or a boy that I could call my friend. When classes were finished, I would go to my room and go to sleep.

Slothfulness casts into a deep sleep, and an idle person will suffer hunger. (Proverbs 19:15 KJV)

One day, I went to my biology class. The class was in the lecture hall. It was a minimum of 499 students in this lecture hall. The girl next to me was talking. The professor stopped the lecture and told me to get out. I was confused because again, there were 499 students. So how can you simply identify me as the one talking? Well, she then turned to press a button on her computer; and before I knew it, my face was on the big screen. She said if necessary, she would call security. Confused as I was, I got up and left. It bothered me, and the day was still young, so I sat outside in the middle of campus for a couple of hours in deep thought. I was getting tired, so I took a different route to my room. As I got to the top of the stairs, there was a round table with three people at it. I looked at them and kept walking. I opened the door. One girl chased after me. She asked me could I be their fourth. I didn't understand what she meant by that, so I said, "No, I am tired, and I do not know what you are talking about." She continued to smile at me, so I smiled back.

She said, "Hi, I am Brownie." (Brownie has the same name as me.) I then let my guard down and said okay. She then screamed with excitement. She brought me back to the table and introduced me to everyone. They needed a fourth to play spades. Now I didn't tell them that I had only ever played a few times; but from that moment, we all became very, very, good friends.

Brownie and I were instant best friends. She was like the half of me that I kept quiet. She was beautiful, bad, and unashamed. But what I loved about her is that she did it with a smile on her face. It was like she would tell people off in the kindest way and finish it with I love you though. Boy, was this intriguing. To her, I was the calm before the storm. She loved me because I was different, super kind but still had my own mind, not driven by the wind, but rugged. She taught me that it is okay to be who I am.

Out of nowhere, people just started introducing themselves to me. People began to invite me to parties: African parties, Jamaican parties, fraternity parties, adult parties, and many more. Every party that I was invited to I went to, which led to this: I found myself at the club Monday because it was ladies' night, Tuesday because it was thirsty Tuesday, Wednesday because it was half off on the entrance, Thursday because it was while N out Thursdays, Fridays because the club was popping, Saturdays because drinks were free after midnight.

My life became parties, sex, drugs, and porn. And if I didn't get it, somebody else had it to give to me.

That light that I had begun to dim. I cared less and less about people and not at all about myself. I began living day to day, numb to the world, numb to my family, and numb to love. I felt no love from anyone until one day. My best friend Nathaniel Rocket came back to town. He called me. I invited him over. We laughed and talked for hours, all the pain, all the numbness, all the loneliness went away. I had previously called him and asked him how to cook rice. When he got there, it was burnt. To this day, we still laugh about it. The time came for me to go to bed. He began to leave. I then told him that he didn't have to go. (Who knew that night would affect us ten years later?) For the first time in our lives, we made sweet apple pie and added some vanilla ice cream on top. It was like the colors of butterflies coming together and making something beautiful. Afterward, we decided that because we loved each other so much it would be best if we remained best friends because neither one of us could stand the thought of losing the other one, and neither one of us was ready to be with each other.

> And it came to pass, when he had made an end of speaking unto Saul, that the soul of Jonathan was knit with the soul of David, band Jonathan loved him as his own soul. (1 Samuel 18:1 KJV)

For a few months, I felt whole. I felt happy. I felt like I was on top of the world sitting on cloud nine. It was like he was my high. So I begin to lose those distasteful things. Spirit of depression, loose me. Spirit of oppression, loose me. Dumb and death spirit, loose me. Spirit of perversion, loose me. And I later found one partner. Alexander Whittmon became my boyfriend. For short, we called him White. White was a cool dude. He was about five feet nine, and the complexion was that of midnight. His teeth was extremely white, and his face was just beautiful to look at. He would often speak Spanish to me in the heat of the moment. He was like my first real boyfriend. Things began to get crazy. Brownie had a dorm room with four rooms in it. I did too. But I moved out of my dorm room into hers. White had an apartment but moved in the room with me. Browine's boyfriend named Boyle moved in the room with her. Brownie's friend Jasmine moved into the next room, but she was talking to White. And the last room was sometimes used for random friends. And so it started up again: parties, sex, drugs, and porn.

As time went on, I realized that White had lost interest in me as did I him. Brownie told me that I should leave him. But as I began to watch them closely, it was almost like White and Brownie had a deep dark secret and wanted me out of the picture. All at once, that numbness began to come back. Before I had looked up, two years had passed, and I was in an unhealthy relationship. I was unhappy, unwanted; but I didn't want to be the one to leave him because during our friendship, he shared with me that his last girlfriend left him for a girl. And that had truly scared him.

During that time, I met this guy. His name was Dean. Dean looked like White but thinner. He was a beautiful Black man...like the definition of tall, dark, and handsome. What separated him from White was his personality. He was so kind to me and wanting nothing in return. He made me feel like I was beautiful, loved, and that he was lucky to be in my presence. His energy was big. The type of energy I hadn't felt before. It was pure. I wanted to be around him, I wanted to be near him, I wanted to smell him, heck... I just wanted him. We end up hanging out almost every night to the point where my friends thought that I was cheating on White with him. But my definition of cheating was physically engaging with someone else while in a relationship with someone else. But now, when I think about it, maybe I was emotionally cheating and didn't realize it. In the short amount of time that I spent with Dean, I fell in love with him. Dean ended up disappearing for a few years. The crazy thing about it is that after we went through life, thirteen years later, he found me again. I was his neighbor, and we don't know where the story ends. Because it's still being written. But he grew up to be some delicious eye candy. So one night, I picked an argument with White, hoping that he would leave me. By the time it was finished, I found out that he had been seeing a Hispanic woman. This crushed me. Because even though I knew it was over, it was actually over. About a week or so passed, and he called me and asked me if he could pick me up. I went along with it. That day was the first time he took me out of house around people. We went on the Dequindre Trail. We grabbed a bite to eat. And then we went back to his place. He apologized for all that he had done to me. And then he properly broke up with me.

I later moved into my first apartment. It was a large studio. It wasn't much, but it was good enough for me. I was so proud that I called the beautiful woman so that she could come and see how good I was doing on my own. I had paid off all my bills for six months. And I had begun to put my energy into school and work. I did not stop partying, but I minimized it. In my mind, I was doing good. If I felt empty, I did schoolwork. If I felt lonely, I would request more hours at work. Things were running smoothly for me, so I thought. The beautiful woman finally made her way to my place. I was happy that that day had come. I had prepared a meal for her, and I had some cards because my family often played a card game called 1500. But when she got there, she had a look of disgust. She did not want any food, and she did not want to play any cards. She looked around and stayed about ten minutes and left. She never returned to that apartment. This hurt, but I knew of one person who could lift my spirit. So I called Nathaniel Rocket. What a benevolent friend. He just so happened to be in town. Now he was not a drinker, but I told him what I was going through. And he brought me a sparkling drink. As always, his presence calmed the atmosphere. Why was he the only man that I could ever see? Why was he so kind to me? Really, who was he?

We made it our mission to always see each other if we were ever in the same city at the same time. As time went on periodically, he would come to visit. It got to a point where almost once a month, Amani Lee-zoni and he would come visit me. But during that time, Brownie had no place to live, so she and Boyle were living with me. I often felt lonely, so I got a cat. Her name was Sam. She was as a little angel. She would often climb up my legs until she made it to my shoulders; and from there, she would chew on my glasses. While she was in my presence, I never felt the urge to do anything distasteful. My apartment became the chill spot. Time went on, and before I knew it, all my friends were playing 1500. We were like a small family. We had our ups and downs, but if anyone tried to come in between us, they were left on the hanging end.

> Bear with one another and, if one has a complaint against another, forgive each other; as the Lord has forgiven you, so you also must forgive. (Colossians 3:13)

> Then I saw a new heaven and a new earth, for the first heaven and the first earth had passed away, and the sea was no more. And I saw the holy city, new Jerusalem, coming down out of heaven from God, prepared as a bride adorned for her husband. And I heard a loud voice from the throne saying, "Behold, the dwelling place of God is with man. He will dwell with them, and they will be his people, and God himself will be with them as their God. He will wipe away every tear from their eyes, and death shall be no more, neither shall there be mourning, nor crying, nor pain anymore, for the former things have passed away." (Revelation 21:1–4 ESV)

CHAPTER 10

This Army Life Is Crazy

Time had elapsed. Day to day, I was living, not able to feel him Smiling down on me. Lord, where are you? So I began searching for him, looking at nature, reading the Scriptures, and listening to his Son. For this was the way. But I thought it was going to be easy. I thought that I would not relapse. For I thought that temptation would flee, not knowing that I had the power to command it to leave.

> But we are not of those who shrink back to
> destruction, but of those who have faith to the
> preserving of the soul. (Hebrews 10:39)

In college, I began to make it my mission not to fail any of my classes. If the time was near and I was failing a class, I would withdraw from the class so that I would not have an F. I did that about five times. During those times, I was going and going but not moving at all. One day, Amani came to town and told me that she was leaving for the Army. I was so confused because she did not even discuss with me that she was joining. In an attempt to make her change her mind and having little knowledge about it, I said to her, "Why would you join an organization just to die?"

She put her head down for a moment, then put her hand on my shoulder and said, "I want you to do some serious research on it for a couple of months. And if the good outweighs the bad, then I will see you sooner than you think."

This caused me to go into somewhat of a depression. Amani was everything to me so much so that when she left me, I could not see my life without her. So I did my research and joined a few months later. Sometime in January of the next year, I joined the United States Armed Forces.

> Have I not commanded you? Be strong and courageous. Do not be afraid; do not be discouraged, for the LORD your God will be with you wherever you go. (Joshua 1:9)

Time had passed and it came to the last week before I shipped out. My first thought was to go and hide out because I was sure that I wanted a change, but I was afraid of the unknown. I had no appetite, and I must have lost about ten pounds because my pants were fitting loose. I questioned actually leaving because leaving meant that I was ready, and I most certainly WAS NOT. Even though my pain ran DEEP, I was accustomed to my life, and I was okay with feeling numb because that was my go-to. I did not want to go because I thought I would become someone else or something else.

The time was approaching, so I invited all my friends over, which was thirteen in all. We played games, we drank JUST JUICE, and we allowed the natural herbs to fill every room. Things got crazy, I mean, really crazy. Before I knew it, all thirteen of us had experienced an increased heart rate, slowed reactions, what we called "smart thoughts" and anger. We played several games throughout the night. And some games required more physical things. But the game that set it off was equivalent to the last bank robbery in the movie *Set It Off*. It just went bad. The game of truth or dare, someone had dared Amani and Boyle to go in the closet for fifteen minutes which caused Brownie and Amani to get into an argument. Amani's sister and friend got into it with Boyle, for he was saying mean things about Brownie. Brownie yelled at everyone, including me. Boyle then, full of anger, got up at 3:00 a.m. and walked outside, which caused

Brownie to chase after him. Before I knew it, everyone was at each other's throats. This was almost the end of the road for Brownie and I. She had said some things that led me to believe that she was never my friend, things that JUST JUICE and natural herbs don't make you say. She had hurt me. It was very personal. But I decided that I would give her one more chance, and I'm glad that I did because later Brownie became my best friend.

Do not run from change, embrace it.

Ship day! The night before, I had to spend the night in a hotel courtesy of the government. They had a pool, fitness room, and free food. Too scared, I decided that sleep would be the best move. The morning came, and he smiled down on me. It was almost like someone was opening a door for me. I had passed the test. I had passed medical. I had passed the physical portion, and I passed the mental portion. They had given me all that I needed and a plane ticket. They then drove me to the airport and dropped me off. This was a change in tempo. For I was completely lost because I had never been in an airport or around that many people that I could remember. Mentally, I began to go into a box. I went to the restroom and began to cry. So I thought about running, but then I remembered what one of the sergeants from the Military Entrance Processing Station (MEPS) said. He said, "You are government property. And if you do not finish your contract the correct way or you cannot adapt, we can and will ruin your life." So I then put on my big girl pants and found someone to help me get to where I was going because you cannot run, especially if they are always watching.

I was twenty years old when I arrived at Ft. Jackson along with about fifty others. In-processing was a bunch of hurrying up and waiting. For a split second, I had thought, *If this is basic training, then this is too easy.* What a rude awakening. We would get up at 6:00 a.m., work out until 7:30 a.m., and have to be dressed by 9:00 a.m. We would be rushed to eat breakfast, then hurry back to the in-processing station and wait. Then we would eat lunch around eleven thirty and hurry and get back to the in-processing station and wait.

This lasted for about one full week. While completing the medical portion of in-processing, I was issued birth-control glasses known as BCGs. They were called BCGs because no one would touch you with a ten feet pole with these glasses because they were twice the size of bifocal glasses. During that in-processing week, I met a girl from Jamaica. Let's call her Ma'ica. Also, a girl who would follow me to my duty station, her name was Jane. Throughout that week, we had about one hour in totaling where we had a small window to get to know each other. Ma'ica was showing off the fact that she was one of the few people who spoke the dialect Patois. But what she didn't know was that I understood some of it because that old Boyle was also Jamaican, and I had been around him for years. Jane was showing off the fact that she could dance. So I told everyone that I was trained in aikido martial arts. Being that I had taken a course in college, I believed that I was trained.

> Be careful of the things that you say because
> you never know how it could come back and bite
> you in the butt.

After in-processing, the drill sergeants told us to pack our bags because we were shipping off to BCT, in other words basic training. So they put us on a bus and told us to cover our faces, and if we decided to look up that our career was going to end before it begins. So of course, I kept my eyes completely closed. But one girl didn't, and I could do nothing but listen with my eyes closed. They stopped the bus and pulled her off. The crazy thing is that I never heard from her or anything else about her. It was as though she simply disappeared. Soon after that, no one remembered her, not even me. I couldn't remember her face, which was odd for me, because I have and had an impeccable picture memory. I could always remember a face but never a name.

There I was, sharing a room with fifty women. This was a different assignment for me. I wasn't used to being this close to that many women. We did everything together: eat, sleep, and shower. Things began to move on a periodic table for us. You had all the elements and their physical properties" a table of the chemical elements arranged in order of atomic number, usually in rows, so that elements with similar atomic structure and hence similar chemical properties appear in vertical columns (*Oxford University, English Dictionary* 2022).

Every morning, I would get up and recite the twenty-third Psalm. I knew that I was in the belly of the beast, and the name of the game was survival of the fittest. I wasn't that physically strong, but I knew how to survive. **Boy, did God keep me. He kept me through all the trials and through the tribulations. He kept me so that I can be a living witness, so that I can spread the good news, so I can do what I am called to do.**

One day, we had a ten-mile run in the morning for PT. It sucked because it was raining. I remember we were the fourth squad to include fifty men, the fifty women, and four drill sergeants. It was raining so hard and loud that you could barely see the person in front of you. This was a hard time I had thought, *Run! Run!* "Don't shed no tears" was the cadences they were chanting. I was so upset that my cry began to make a sound. But as I looked around, 99 percent of us were feeling the same way. Normally we would finish at seven thirty, but this day was finished at eight thirty. We got back to the barracks. No one said anything, I mean, no one had anything to say to anyone. Were we exhausted mentally and physically. That day of many broke us. But that's the motto, "Army strong." So what they had to do was break us down mentally and physically so that they could build us into a rifleman?

Rifleman, Rifleman! We had become riflemen, mindless vessels who could only do as told but could not think. If we were told to organize the rocks outside, well, the rocks outside got organized. Whatever we were told to do, we did without thinking twice. But this is why it is crucial that the drill sergeants that are selected for those positions have/had been completely screened, and they absolutely have no desire to sleep with the soldiers because soldiers will do as told without question.

On this day, the drill sergeants wanted to mess with us. They came on the loudspeaker and told all the men to meet the women in the women's sleeping area. They wanted men on one side and women on the other side in alphabetical order. This was called "toeing the line." They said that they needed us to have some motivation, so they made us do the "Movator." The Movator consists of heel toes, jumping jacks in place, while repeating after the drill sergeant at various speeds. We did that for about an hour until one of the men passed out. Afterward, they allowed us to sit down where we were and eat lunch. In front of me were two guys who looked alike and had similar last names. One was loud and made sexual gestures, and the other looked really mean. At that moment, I remembered the dream that I had. And I was completely in tune. I told myself that I am supposed to be right where I am. And where I was in the United States Army. **At that time, I didn't realize that God had paved the way for me. For I was still a babe in Christ putting together pieces of the puzzle but not being able to see the whole story. Just believing my instinct and believing that God wouldn't have put me here if I didn't belong, that was faith.**

One day, we got up and did PT. On this day, we did a full-body workout. We did intervals of pull-ups, push-ups, sit-ups, and lunges for hours. Once we finished and got dressed for the day, we did drill and ceremony exercises for half of the day which means we had to learn how to move our unit from one place to another in an orderly manner and learn all the steps in between. This was done in the HOT sun, in the heart of South Carolina. We were the definition of *exhausted*. Once we finished that, for the rest of the day, we learned how to build tents. They let us stop for breaks to eat and use the restroom if needed, but we had a full day. So when it was time for bed, we all passed out. Four thirty in the morning arrived. The drill sergeants came in screaming, "GET UP, YOU DIRTY FILTHY, SOLDIERS." They stood by the bathroom and the exit. And they said, "Toe the line." I immediately ran to the bathroom, but my drill sergeant yelled for me to stop. So in midair, I stopped. I said to the drill sergeant, I really have to go. She told me to get back in line. I screamed and said, "DRILL SERGEANT, I CAN'T HOLD IT."

She then screamed back and said, "YOU WILL HOLD IT IF I SAY so." The next thing you know is that they said do the motivator. At that moment, 30 cc times 50 cc of urine started to pour out of me. It was so much that the other soldiers started running away. And the drill sergeant looked at me and put her head down and said, "Clean this up and go to bed." My Spidey senses suggested that she felt horrible. But that incident made things better and worse for me on the same note. On one if I had to go to the restroom, I was automatically granted access to a bathroom with no hesitation. But on another note, I was known as the girl who peed her pants. So the drill sergeants and soldiers teased me. That went on for quite some time.

> And we know that in all things God works for the good of those who love him, who have been called according to his purpose. (Romans 8:28)

Quite some time had passed, and I was still in BCT. I had got into a routine of working out at this time, eating breakfast at that time, and going on about the day as directed. Well, on this day, after we got dressed for the day, the drill sergeant came in and said it was combatives day. I thought, *Okay, well, I guess they are going to teach us how to fight.* To my surprise, they showed us one move and one position. They showed us how to grab someone if they were reaching for us. Now everyone had to perform the same two moves, when it was my turn, the female drill sergeant started to yell, saying, "She said she was trained in aikido." So all the drill sergeants ran over to watch me fight. I was confused because they only taught us one move. They also said that if we hurt our opponent or do a move that they didn't teach, then we would be kicking ourselves out of the Army. So I did the moves that they had just taught us and got my opponent to fall to her knees. So I won the fight right! But my drill sergeant didn't see it like that. She got up and said this was a complete waste of time. And when she left, so did the other spectators. Boy, did that make me feel bad. Because even though she was mean to me, I wanted to make her proud. She was like my drill sergeant mom—well, in a long thought of a theory. Okay, maybe not, but she was someone whom I felt was mean to me because she had to train me not because she hated me. We were getting close to the end, and we had a PT test. This was where they would test to see if we could run two miles in a certain time, do a certain amount of push-ups and sit-up all in a certain time. Well, I was nervous because I always hated tests. But I got out there, and for the first time, I was light as a butterfly. I was as fast a baseball player running to home base after catching a ball somewhere out in left field. I passed! I was so happy! I screamed and was in good spirits the remainder of that day. Drill sergeant, she almost cried. She was so happy for me. I felt like nothing could bring me down. Nothing could bring me down, until something brought me down. So the drill sergeants were happy because we had a 99 percent pass rate. They let us have the day to sit and talk to the guys. Then out of nowhere, a bird flew into the barracks. The barracks were our living quarters, the voice, the voice that was the feeling, "the Lord." He said to me that things are going to get a lot harder before they get easier. All of a sudden, I started sweating profusely, and it looked as though I was going to pass out. My drill sergeant, she came over to me and said, "You are going to get through this. Go get some water and fresh air." It was like she heard him talking to me. But how could he be talking to me and her at the same time about me?

> My sheep hear my voice, and I know them,
> and they follow me. I give them eternal life, and
> they will never perish, and no one will snatch
> them out of my hand. (John 10:27–28 ESV)

There were a few sayings from the Army that stuck with me throughout life, like, "If you don't know anything, then remember this. Don't mess with the human resources or the cooks because they can mess you over ten times as hard. And the hardest thing about being in the Army is taking the PT test."

One day, it was known that we had to take our PT test. This was the final test we had to take before we could move on to AIT (advanced individual training). The female drill sergeants were out of the office that day. So we were left with the male drill sergeants. One of them in particular was Drill Sergeant BeckBack. He was a Caucasian male. Throughout my time there, he made sure I knew that he didn't like me. He would say things like you remind me of my ex-wife who is a female dog, or "You are stupid," or, "You are the epitome of ugly." What he must have known is that I had already believed that to be true about myself because I never said anything back to him but "Yes, Drill Sergeant."

He was so mean to me that one day, we had a free day. On this day, we were going to put on a show for the drill sergeants. All the guys got with all the girls, and we were going to show off some creative drill and ceremony with all that we had learned. Well, one of the guys said, "Let's mock, Drill Sergeant BeckBack, you know, 'cause he is always messing with Lavondo." They laughed and began practicing. I had looked down with tears in my eyes because in actuality, they were making fun of me. A person I considered to be my friend to this day said, "Hey y'all, let's not do that because it could be offensive." His name was Eastbook. Did I mention that we were known by our last names?

The day of the Final PT test. I was so nervous that I couldn't remember my techniques, and I couldn't remember what was left and what was right. It came down to me. I was up. It was my time to shine. Well, I nailed my push-ups, and I nailed my sit-ups. My final task was to run. So I got ready. "They say stay ready so that you don't have to get ready." As soon as they gave us the approval, I ran. But it seemed like I was running in slow motion, and it seemed like I could see myself running in slow motion. Before I knew it, Drill Sergeant BeckBack started screaming, "You fat, stupid, black female dog. I know you aren't going to make it. YOU CAN'T MAKE IT, AND YOU WON'T MAKE IT with your ugly tail." If suicide was a factor, he would have been the reason that I committed the ultimate sin. I was out loud crying like I had lost the love of my life, crying so hard that others were alarmed. The whole way back to the barracks, he made me feel lower than low, telling me how they are getting ready to prepare the paperwork to chapter me out of the Army. We finally arrived back, and he went in and told all the soldiers and all the drill sergeants that I had failed and this was a failure to adapt. So they could kick me out for that reason.

After the tears, I had no words for anyone. I had accepted my fate. This wasn't the place for me. So the next day, the first sergeant called me to his office. He said, "Did you pass your PT test?"

I said "Drill Sergeant BeckBack said I didn't, so I guess I didn't."

He then stared at me with this questionable glare. He then told me to leave. So I did as I was told. Later that day, another drill sergeant, woman from another platoon pulled me aside and said, "I know what happened because when he had you out there, I was out there as well. So don't worry but be completely honest if someone asks you what happened. Tell it all."

I responded, "Yes, Drill Sergeant." The day went on as regular. The next day or so, the first sergeant, the commander, and all my drill sergeants, plus the female drill sergeant that approached me, called me into the office. The first sergeant said, "Lavondo, I am going to ask you one last time what happened when you were taking your PT test." So I told them everything exactly what he said, exactly how he made me feel, and exactly what happened. He then said, "Okay. I need you to leave this office."

I said, "Yes, First Sergeant." I was calm and began to smile and chat a little with the few friends that I had made.

It had seemed like hours had passed. They called me back into the office, and Drill Sergeant BeckBack apologized for harassing me.

He then said, "We will not be moving forward with a chapter, and you do not have to retake the PT test." And to top it off, he asked me what I would like to see happen.

I said, "I would like you to tell all the soldiers that I have passed my PT test."

He said, "Okay, please leave this office."

I was so happy the moment I closed the door, I began screaming in tears of joy. Everyone asked, "What's going on? What's going on?" So I said I can't get into details, but I actually passed the PT test. This was crazy because what was going on behind closed doors? Who knew that I was the example? Who knew that because of me, many wrongs would be righted? Who knew that I was right where I was supposed to be BUT GOD. GLORY, GLORY TO THE MOST HIGH.

> For I know the plans I have for you, declares
> the Lord, plans for welfare and not for evil, to give
> you a future and a hope. (Jeremiah 29:11 ESV)

Time had rolled around for me to graduate basic training. I was so happy that someone like me could pass. No, I was happy that I passed because I had been through a lot and I had said a lot. But what about the things I didn't say, like, where was my Dad (as I digress but not really)? Well, I had contacted my family a few weeks earlier and gave them the date and time of the graduation. No one showed up, not one. Wait. Wait. Wait, with ten minutes left for visitation, guess who showed up? My dad! So where was my dad? He was doing everything in his power to get back to his children. This was something that went in my history book. He made me feel like I was the luckiest girl in the world with the best dad ever. **It's the little things that mean the most**. And to this day, he never lets me forget that I am.

After BCT (basic training), all of us went on to AIT (advanced individual training). This was simply schooling for our job. I went to human resources school. It was quite different from basic training. We got up, did PT, ate breakfast, started class, then went to lunch, then afterward got back to class. Once the school day was finished, which was at 5:00 p.m. daily, we were able to go to dinner and get to know fellow 42As (human resources specialist). We had fifty guys and fifty girls going to school for the same thing. Automatically, this was amazing. For every one girl, there was one guy. I had begun talking to this guy. His name was Jid. (This was crazy because my love and pain stories will come from a guy or guys whose first names begin with the letter J. I think the story of my life is to avoid men whose names start with that letter. But I didn't know that during this time.) He was six feet five, 150 lbs. of muscle, hazel eyes, the complexion of a skinny mocha with chocolate shaving on top. If I were to assume, I would have assumed that his BMI was at 4 percent. So you can only imagine how fit he really was. He found me to be different from what he said. I could only imagine how beautiful our babies would be. We talked every night and sat next to each other during the day so much so that the sergeants made it their business to follow us and listen in if we were talking. It got to appoint where the other girls were noticing, and girls did as they do and started drama. They didn't feel that I was pretty enough. This chick whom I thought was my friend (the story of my life) came in like a wrecking ball. She was like Rapunzel.

She let down her long hair and started speaking Spanish, and before I knew it, he was no longer interested in me. She later apologized for taking my man. But I told her that "there was no need to apologize because if he'll leave me that quickly, imagine what he'll do to you." A year or so later, they ended up with a child together, and he left her for the next best thing. (Karma, karma, it could be bad, or it could be good. But that depends on you. But that's neither here nor there.)

At this point, we are still in AIT. And we have to test every day to see if we are retaining the knowledge. Well, it wasn't that I didn't understand or that it was hard. What was difficult was the time we had to research the answers. Every question required a researched answer that you only had a few seconds to answer. So fine Sergeant Bill recognized that I was struggling with the course. He would sometimes give me the test a second time or an alternate test. Well, it was getting close to the end, and grades were due. So he said while chatting with a fellow soldier that "there will be no one who fails in my class." To my knowledge, I was the only one who could have been failing. The soldier looked at me, so I took a deep breath. I then knew it was me who was failing. A few minutes later, our first sergeant came into the class and asked for the grades. He then said, "Congratulations to each and every one of you for passing the mental portion of AIT."

> Do not forget to show hospitality to strangers, for by so doing some people have shown hospitality to angels without knowing it. (Hebrews 13:2 NIV)

During AIT, I met two friends. One name was Borevile, and the other one was Peacedinger. These two understood the assignment. With no hesitation or confusion, they were my friends. They lifted me up during hard times, stood by my side during questionable times, and had my back during difficult times. I remember one night, we had a creative night. This meant that everyone with some talent could show off some skills. We had belly dancers, singers, rappers, and poets. I had decided that I would let some people in or maybe just let them scratch the surface with some of me. So I read to them a poem that I wrote many years earlier called "Love in the Bloody Chamber."

Love in the Bloody Chamber 2.0.

She was only seventeen, with high hopes and big dreams
Married for materialistic things not realizing his plans for guillotine
She left the house for school, but she left too SOON
She left as a babe but a Woman is what came back
She had been dragged through the grave and beat down, that's a fact
She married a man whose definition of love was distorted

He was in the closet, confused, and cold-hearted
With the two hundred bodies found, you
might as well call him a Murderer
But not the typical kind just the emotional
Oh…how this pained Mom's heart
Her youngest child living in the dark

As Peacedinger and Borevil said…this was not love
But the Good Lord above swooped down, gave me safe passage,
Handed me a pamphlet, full of information
And removed me from that situation

Poem by Britteny Lavondo

One night, the sergeant came in our room at 4:00 a.m., screaming, "GET OUT OF BED." So with the quickness, we all jumped up almost in sequence. But I started running. The sergeants yelled, "WHAT ARE YOU DOING?"

I said, "I have to pee, and I can't hold it."

They said, "HOLD it."

I said, "Sergeant, respectful I can't." Then I remember tears started falling from my face as I shook, and Jane covered her mouth. And her eyes started watering for she remembered the embarrassment that I had just faced in BCT. The sergeants then started asking where the men were. All of us had the same responses. "Uhm, I guess in the men's rooms."

They said, "We are here because we heard intimate sounds."

The girls started laughing and said that "Lavondo made those sounds while she was asleep." They then allowed me to go to the restroom. I was thankful that I was able to make it because mother nature had said hello.

A few days had passed. By this time, my hair was rolled up tighter than some of today's young guy's jeans. It was tight so much so that the water bounced off my hair. I guess my roots finally decided to show. At this point, I was still learning about the military rank and structure. So one day, I asked one of the other sergeants if I could go and get my hair done. He looked at me and said, "Where they do that at?" My argument was that graduation was coming, and I looked like a man. He laughed and said no. I put my head down and walked away.

The next day, he wasn't there, so I asked one of the female sergeants. And she said, "Take your battle buddy Borevile, and remember I didn't say yes." So I and my buddy walked to the subway that was about a ten-minute walk away. Then we went to the hair shop to get my hair done. It only took about five hours, so we were making good timing. We got back to the installation at the same time as the other sergeant. It was as though everyone could see the steam that was coming from his head. He was the definition of *mad*. He had never cursed at us until that moment.

He demanded that we come to his office immediately. He said, "I am so mad that I could kick y'all out of the Army right now and ruin the rest of y'all's life. Why would you, you Lavondo, disobeyed a direct order? If I am telling you something, it is for a reason. The place you went to is off-limits because they are under government watch and anything at any time could have gone down. I am responsible for your safety. Do you think I want to go visit your mom and have to explain to her that I let you out of my sight for one day and you got killed because you decided to disobey a direct order?" Boy, did he make me feel bad. By the end of that conversation, I had told him everything. He told us to get out and don't pass go, don't collect $200, but go directly to our living quarters while he and the female sergeant discussed our punishment. The next day, we heard no word; so we ate breakfast, lunch, and dinner. And after each one, we came back to our room.

The next day came around, we ate breakfast and lunch and went back to our room. Somewhere between lunch and dinner, he and the other sergeant came with our punishment. They said, "Since you all are about to graduate, you two will not be able to take leave to go home, get a day pass for family and friends, get a day off post, and you must paint all the walls." We humbly accepted our fates because it could have been worse.

Over the next few weeks, we painted the walls. We ate breakfast, ate lunch, and ate dinner. In between times, we painted the walls. We had gotten to a point of contentment. We were okay. But quickly we learned that the punishment that we had was the thing that saved us. The nights came where everyone could have a day pass and family and friends, and they could go off post. Well, all the girls had secretly met up with all the guys at a hotel. The girls were very cute. They had their hair down or curled. This was amazing because none of us had seen the others dress up or outside of uniform. The guys were, of course, dressed to impress. They were fly. The sergeants then gave all of us a safety brief. Once everyone left the premises, Borevile and I decided to have a two-man party. We cut on some music that was on our phones and began to dance while we were painting the walls. That night, I learned a lifelong lesson. Painting walls is not for me. No, but seriously, what the devil sought of for bad **God made good.** That night, I found a lifelong friend. The night went on, and Borevile and I were directed to put the paint brushes down and head to our night quarters.

The next day, around 6:00 a.m., everyone began to come back. But they did not look as good as they looked when they left. Some of the women's make-up was smeared all over their faces. Others' wigs were hanging off. Others' clothing was wrecked of vomit. Others just looked drained. Jamaica came in, screaming and crying. She was in such a disarray that the sergeants came to her aid. They set her down and asked what was going on. She couldn't speak right, and she was going in circles. After five minutes of trying to unscramble what she was saying, they finally grabbed her by the arms and shook her a little bit and said, "If you don't tell us what happened, we cannot help you." She then took a deep breath and said something along the lines like, "All the females met up with the males in a hotel. We all drank beverages that elevated us all night. As the night increased, all the guys became cute to the girls, and all the girls became sexy to the guys. Everyone laid with a partner of the opposite sex, everyone including me." She then burst out into tears crying loudly.

So the sergeants then repeated to her what she had just said. And they asked her if it was forced. She said no. They then said okay and took deep breaths. Then they said, "Was this your first time?" She replied no. They sat with puzzled looks all over their faces.

She then said, "I'm married, and protection was not a question that was on our minds. They then made her call her husband and explain the situation to him. That was a sad day. Later we ended up finding out that forty to of the fifty girls were pregnant. Based on that, they have new policies in place now. This was an interesting time to be pregnant because it was at the tail end of the Iraqi freedom war. **This reminded me of how Joseph believed that God would use him in a leadership role as he was revealed in a dream. But his brothers sold him into slavery, then lied to their father Israel. Joseph faced many hardships but never doubted God. He later became in second command from the Pharaoh. He was the second most powerful person who ended up ultimately saving his whole family. See, what was meant for bad God used for good. But God!**

The time had come for all of us to go our separate ways. This was harder than joining the military. Leaving your friends felt like you were losing a piece of yourself. It was tough. Because Borevile and I had gotten in trouble, we were denied leave. We had to go to our installations and put in leave with them after thirty days of our arrival. I went to Ft. Carson. Borevile did not follow me there, but Jane did. Upon my arrival, the first thing I noticed was that I was having trouble breathing. I later found out that Colorado is like three thousand feet above sea level. So I had to acclimate to the air. After I was in-processed, my organization came to pick me up. They had another soldier in the car, and they said don't speak to her. So I didn't speak.

On day one, I had an interview with the commander. He said, "We only have three females, and I can't take another attitude. Why should you be a part of this team? Do you have an attitude problem?" This was definitely shocking to me because it made me question whether or not race and gender is a problem.

I took a big gulp and said, "Most people get the wrong idea. Not all of us are the same. I can assure you that if an attitude is present, that you will know the reason why, and I don't have any problems." He glared at me as I gave him a polite face.

He then said, "If you join this team, you cannot talk to PVT [private first class] Longwin."

I said, "Okay, but if you don't mind me asking, why not?"

He said, "Because she is a bad seed." As we all know, cats are curious. PVT Longwin was a beautiful young girl born and raised in Mississippi. She was super pretty, but she was the epitome of ATTITUDE. Her attitude would flip from zero to one hundred real quick. And everybody, I mean, everybody that was in the path of her, rage got Sucker punched with a loaded 9 mm gun. This didn't bother me much because I had a sister whose medulla oblongata was a little enlarged as well, so her attitude didn't bother me much. I admired her because she wasn't afraid to live and be herself. She absolutely didn't care what anyone thought. See, I didn't require an explanation. I required communication, and she required a no-judgment zone; therefore, we became good friends. Hanging with her helped visualize the good relationship that my sister and I could have. (In visualizing that, it came true. Right now today, my sister is my best friend.) She made me feel happy, loved, and wanted. She even helped me to feel pretty at times. See, my confidence wasn't extremely low or extremely high, so a boost every now and again wasn't bad. It was like she had to go through some of the pain so that she could help me. I don't think she ever really knew how much she helped me. Without a shadow of a doubt, wherever she is, I will always love her.

Beautiful Woman

Did you know that you are beautiful?
Look into your own eyes, not through the man,
Woman or thing looking through the rose-
colored glasses back at you
Remember the you who believed that you were something special
Remember the you who had thoughts of being successful
Or happy or maybe even thoughts of you
being married with a family
Oh beautiful girl
Please don't give up for life is going to happen
Winds are going to blow left, right, up, and down
So you have to be STEADFAST and STAND your GROUND
You have to be strong even when the wind is calm
See the foundation was already paved but
it is up to you to build upon
Oh, beautiful girl…
When your personality comes to serve
The energy of your soul begins to glow
So don't let your light dim or
Let it put you in some mental hole
For your purpose is far greater than your SITUATIONAL
Beautiful Women
Beautiful Women
BEAUTIFUL WOMAN
The time is now for you to start becoming
That beautiful WOMAN
Understand that Beauty starts within
Hey, beauty, over there, I love your hair
Hey, beauty, over there I love your smell
So let those random compliments a day begin to
Propel and guide you on your way
Let's stop JUDGING and start getting to know…
Did you know that your test could potentially save HER
It starts with a simple, kind gesture or even a compliment a day

But wait…
Here is a little test
Pay attention and you'll see how I will not digress
Did you know that 365 days of the year, I wear a new pair of socks?
Did you know that I have had ten dads and five moms?
Did you know that my grandmother was a
Caucasian woman who despised
Of African Americans?
Did you know that my twenty-two-year-
old-sister is actually my daughter?
Did you know that none of those are my truths?
The truth is that I am a beautiful woman
just like each and every one of you
Sometimes I walk with my head down and I may need a boost
Just like each and every one of you
So I leave you with this…
Remember your mother, your sister, your
auntie, or that random woman
Who inspired you,
No, remember you!
For I too am a beautiful woman just like you.

Poem by Britteny Lavondo

That's just that. The Army was a hard but necessary point in my life. I learned so many things, I shed so many tears, I helped so many people, I shed so much blood, I did so many questionable things, I met so many people, I did what I was told, I learned some manners, I learned about partying Monday through Saturday, going to church with a hangover on Sundays, I learned my limits, I learned how to be a single mother, I lived. But one thing I *never* did was forget God. *I stood on his promises. I claimed everything that I had lost. I believed and received.* Most soldiers don't get the opportunity that presented itself to me. There I stood at the age of twenty-six, retired with a full pension only after serving four years. *Glory to God!* My son Eden, who was two at that time, was my new beginning. He changed my life for the better. *Thank you, Father, for opening my womb, after doctors had said I could not have any children. Thank you for my beautiful gift. He is truly something special. Father, I ask that keep your angels kept about him and let no harm, hurt, or danger come his way. Father, I ask that you continue to use me as your vessel so that I can continue to do your will. Be my ears, my eyes, and my tongue. And, Father, I ask that you let this message be divided as many times as possible to those children, to those women, to those men. Let them know that they are not alone, and nor have they ever been, that they must go through the pain, to find their passion, and to walk in their purpose. Father, let them know that you are with them. Thank you, Father, in Jesus's name, Amen.*

Oh, I forgot to mention that I end up in long term relationship with a guy that I had met in the military. For ten years, he abused me mentally, emotionally, and sexually. I can say that I have been through somethings and gained some tough skin. Thank God for removing me from that situation and for that term. It was a hard term, but I did it, and I am a better woman because of it. There is a lot of things that I could say, but "we don't talk about Bruno" (*Encanto*, 2021).

Who knew that it would be up to my auntie Web and I to keep the family and friends in a web of prayers. We speak life, prosperity, peace, and many more things over their lives. We ask God to forgive them for they not know what they do. We are the teachers and the examples. God lights the path and shows us. We then hold the family hands and walk with them down the path. But God…

Thoughts and Feelings

Do you know who you are? Do you know your purpose? Do you know your father? Do you fit in? See, the story of my life is I never fit in. I did not fit in at school. I did not fit in at home. I did not fit in at work. I did not know who I was and wanted for nothing but to be normal. But what is being normal? One of my old pastors once said, "Why fit in when we were made to stand out?" At a young age, I thought that I was the only person going through the test. I felt like my mother did not want me which caused me to seek attention in the wrong places. I felt that my dad was not there, which caused me to end good relationships and prolong bad ones because I did not have my father there teaching me how to love a man or receive love from a man. I felt my sister had a strong dislike for me, and because she was my sister and I felt this way about her, it caused me not to allow anyone to get close to me. I felt that my brother just wasn't there. This caused me to block certain emotions. Not to mention, I was facing a spiritual battle, and I did not know how to win and a victim of generational curses. Boy did I think I was going crazy. I did not think I was going to make it.

But one day, out of nowhere, the **Lord** said to me, "The devil would not try so hard to get you if you weren't as important to me as you are." At that moment, a light bulb went off. **I was wrong**. I was so wrong. It wasn't that my mom did not want me. But I did not walk in my mother's shoes. I did not live her life. I did not have to raise three children by myself. I did not know that my mother saw so much in me that she thought I would become her. She was and is everything to me. What a beautiful woman. Yes, my mommy. It wasn't that my dad wasn't there. It was just he was dealing with things, and he could not be around us until he was delivered. It wasn't that my sister had a strong dislike for me. It was that she wanted to protect me. It wasn't that my brother was not there. It was that he knew that worrying about a situation was not going to change it.

(If you feel like you don't fit in, it's okay because you were created to be the light. And if you do fit in, that means that you are conforming or that you have conformed to darkness. The world that we live in is the darkness. Do you know where you belong? Or where is your home? This country is not your home. Where you currently reside is not your home. Your home is the kingdom which is called New Jerusalem. We do not know why God allows us to go through the things that we go through in life. But what we do know that he has called each and every one of us to edify the kingdom. Let that thing you went through become your testimony. Let that thing save, heal, and deliver the next man, woman, or child. Think of life as putting together a puzzle. At first, it looks to be broken; but once all the pieces come together, it is something beautiful. I am something beautiful, and so are you! See, there are three stages of life. You are either going through something, coming out of something, or about to go through something. With knowledge about that, I bestow upon you this life-altering information. If you have breath in your body, repent, asking the Lord to help you understand who you are, better yet, ask the Lord to help you to better understand who he is. Ask him what is your purpose and then walk in your purpose. Ask the Lord how you can be more like him, and watch the Lord work. Go through the pain, find your passion, and walk in your purpose. And if the first time doesn't work, you may have to do it again and again until you have learned your lesson.

> I have given them thy word; and the world hath hated them, because they are not of the world, even as I am not of the world. I pray not that thou shouldest take them out of the world, but that thou shouldest keep them from the evil. (John 17:14–15 KJV)

Life Lessons

- Keep God first in all of your decisions.
- Understand that being a Christian does not mean life is going to be easy.
- Trust the process.
- Learn how to cook.
- Become independent, not dependent.
- Find out who you are.
- Find out what your purpose is.
- Walk in your purpose.
- Find a hobby.
- Love with no stipulations.
- Give with no consequences.
- It doesn't matter what people think; just be yourself.
- No matter what, always love and respect your parents and remember that they are your parents for a reason.

- Remember that you are enough.
- Remember that we are all created in God's image. And because of that, he says that you are beautiful, and I confirm it.
- Remember to laugh and play because time will come that you can no longer do those things.
- But most importantly, remember to pray, repent, and believe.

ABOUT THE AUTHOR

The author was a young girl who faced many hardships, a young girl who was abused by loved ones, forced into sex, a victim of generational curses, who was mentally, physically, and emotionally broken. But she always had God with her. She overcame her pain, she found her passion, and she is walking in her purpose. For she is a warrior in the army of the Lord.